T0171451

The Way I See It

Grace Guthrie

Illustrations by R. D. S.

WestBow
PRESS
A DIVISION OF THOMAS NELSON

WestBow Press books may be ordered through booksellers or by contacting:

WestBow Press
A Division of Thomas Nelson
1663 Liberty Drive
Bloomington, IN 47403
www.westbowpress.com
1-(866) 928-1240

Because of the dynamic nature of the Internet, any web addresses or links contained in this book may have changed since publication and may no longer be valid. The views expressed in this work are solely those of the author and do not necessarily reflect the views of the publisher, and the publisher hereby disclaims any responsibility for them.

Any people depicted in stock imagery provided by Thinkstock are models, and such images are being used for illustrative purposes only.

Certain stock imagery © Thinkstock.

ISBN: 978-1-4497-7687-9 (sc)
ISBN: 978-1-4497-7688-6 (hc)
ISBN: 978-1-4497-7686-2 (e)

Library of Congress Control Number: 2012921931

Printed in the United States of America

WestBow Press rev. date: 11/28/2012

For my husband, Marty, and my two boys, Casey and Kenny

I can see, and that is why I can be happy, in what you call the dark, but which to me is golden. I can see a God-made world, not a manmade world.

—Helen Keller

Contents

Illustrations

*To view the illustrations in full color and the animation videos of the dreams, please point at them with your smart phone using a QR code scanner app. or you can go to my website: www.letgracebewithyou.com/color/

Foreword

Grace Guthrie came to me with unflagging attention and without an iota of judgment.

I was afraid I wouldn't be able to pay my bills. I was afraid I wouldn't be able to find another job after being laid off for the third time in three years. I was afraid I'd have to move into someone's basement because I couldn't even afford to rent a small apartment. I was afraid I'd entered one of those nightmare moments from which you never recover.

I was absolutely and unequivocally overwhelmed. Everything suddenly seemed too complicated, and I was having trouble thinking about what to do. God sent an angel to feed and nourish Elijah; He sent Grace to encourage and strengthen me.

Grace chases Jesus with a passion that is far too uncommon today. Grace would come by just to check on me, as she knew I wasn't eating well. She refused to let me fall into a funk of faithless thinking by continually encouraging me with God's Word, sometimes even rebuking me when I slipped into thinking someone other than God could be my deliverer.

You hold in your hands many of the same lessons Grace taught me as she helped me back into a deep faith in Christ. Her message is that we must be wholly and totally dependent upon Jesus, and I have watched in amazement as Grace has lived that out in her life. This book is a reminder that there can be no compromise as we follow Jesus to become the person God created us to be.

The theological insights you will discover in this book will bless you, but they are all the more amazing when you understand that Grace is simply a woman with an open Bible and an open heart who takes the time to listen to what God is saying to her.

You will be challenged by Grace, but you will soon see that you have nowhere else to go except to God—and to follow Him with every piece of your heart and every particle in your being is the only way to the abundant life Jesus says we can live now and today. Jesus will bring you to a choice as you read this book: Will you follow Him into a deeper faith, or will you choose to stay independent of Him?

May God grant you grace as you make that decision.

—Jon Walker, Author, *Breakfast with Bonhoeffer* and *Costly Grace*

Acknowledgments

This book is the most humbling experience and act of obedience I have ever displayed in my life.

I thank God for choosing me as a "foolish thing" (1 Cor. 1:27) to make His mighty voice heard once more in times like these.

I thank my husband, Marty, for supporting each step of this mind-blowing journey. I thank him for putting up with the restless nights when I'd wake up to write and for listening to the endless dreams and visions and strangeness that comes from being in the presence of God's spirit.

I thank my two sons, Casey and Kenny, who believed in me.

I thank Beck Sharp and Terrence Boyce for making my outlandish rambling into a book.

I thank Jon Walker and Kathy Sharp for being a supportive force behind my words.

I thank Dr. Eric Stamper for reviewing my book to ensure the scientific facts were accurate.

I thank Allen and Jamie Hamilton for allowing me to hide in their cabin and write.

I thank my dear friends Jeanette Holt and Maria Elena Lopez for their unconditional and supportive friendship.

And thanks to my sister from another mister, Lori Birckhead, who listened to my never-ending insights and "crazy-gracie" babblings with steadfast responsiveness and without a speck of judgment.

Thanks.

Our Eyes

Opinion is holding something to be provisionally true which you do not know to be false.

—Saint Bernard

For most of us, our vision is our dominant sense. We rely on what our eyes see; it is said that 80 percent of what we learn is through the information our eyes irradiate to our brains about the world around us. It is from that perception, that sense, that we collect experiences. We form opinions and certain attitudes based on what we see.

But the way I see it, our vision may be unreliable. What we do with the information passed from eyes to brain mostly depends on our personal perspective. No two people see an object in quite the same way. There is a reason mankind has constantly speculated about the nature of reality. The human race has spent endless hours—years, even centuries—debating about what is real. The conclusion, thus far, is that reality is subjective or may not even exist.

The Mechanism

Our eyes are one of God's masterpieces. The human eye is a complex sensory organ that collects light reflected off objects, bends it, focuses it, and sends information to the brain about the texture, color, and distance of those objects. It is composed of more than *two million* working parts, and the muscles that move the eye are the strongest in the body. Our eye muscles move about a hundred thousand times a day, even when we are sleeping.

However, in order to see—even with these marvels of divine engineering—we must have light. The correlation between the shape of our eye and the intensity of the light determines whether we see things clearly or in a blurry haze. Light goes into the cornea (the "window of the eye") and reflects back to the retina the information gathered by 126 million nerve cells. I find it interesting that the crossed-over rays produce an upside-down image in the retina. This is true of our spiritual vision too. Our earthly eyes have turned upside down what He meant to be perfect, giving us a blurry vision of reality, confusing and distracting us from what God wants us to see. So is anything we see with our carnal eyes real? What if what is *unseen* by our eyes is a more reliable, unchangeable, absolute reality?

Even the brain, the most important organ in the human body (and probably the most complex biological structure in the universe), is obviously unreliable. The information about color, shape, movement, position, and size are all processed separately; there is no area in which they all come together in the brain. So no one can pinpoint physically the location of our consciousness. And if the information that my brain receives from my vision is in any way ambiguous, my brain will fill in the blanks, resulting in optical illusions. How, then, can I trust in my own reality? Or anyone else's?

Perhaps God is trying to tell us that, in spite of the complexity of our eyes and the marvelous capacity of our brains, our eyesight does not compare to the simplicity and accuracy of our heart-sight. We are trying to find the source of our reality—but can we? Are we looking at nothing but our own wrong perception, reflected again and again, distorting objective reality beyond comprehension? Subjective reality is nothing but an opinion, in my opinion.

Quantum Physics and the Spirit

At the very beginning of this journey, one of the terms the Spirit of God gave me to research was *quantum physics*. To my astonishment, I was in a totally unfamiliar but extremely fascinating new world. I was surprised to learn that physicists were far from having found answers to the ultimate question of reality. According to the double-slit experiment, matter apparently acts like matter only when it is "observed." Therefore, the presence of an "observer" has radical implication on the outcome of the matter's own existence.

Everything around us is composed of particles of matter. Including us! Therefore, an eluding portal opens up to a number of hypotheses about the existence of matter.

Quantum physics has also stated that the universe is made of energy, space, mass, and time, and that all these entities interpenetrate each other. I am discovering that I may just have another characteristic of my Creator who has created me in His image. I can "cocreate" my own reality as long as I draw my inspiration from His perfect creation.

My own experiences in the past few years have led me to the conclusion that there *is* a reality beyond my own subjective opinion, one that is being slowly revealed to me through acts of obedience. I feel like I have tuned into a new frequency of consciousness. God is trying to show me realities that are in front of us all but have been hidden until now by the cloaking devices of sin and pride.

God has gifted humans with the highest form of consciousness. We think, and we are aware of the fact that we think. Most animals see a stranger when they look in the mirror. Humans are the rare exception, as we see ourselves. Some scientists—in search of easy answers that pack life's mysteries into a nice, solid, measurable box—have wondered whether free will is nothing more than learned brain activity, a mere result of past experiences. I dare to disagree.

I believe we, as the Bible says, are composed of body, soul, *and* spirit. An average human in denial refuses to believe in this simple concept, so they spend their lives, energy, and resources proving that they can *think* and ignoring the more ethereal aspects of life. This open-minded, self-sufficient, proud attitude brings contradictory results. It causes people to keep their eyes closed without hope and conduct an endless search for what is right in front of them. Only those with "narrow" minds, those who allow God's divine light to flood their consciousness, are allowed a magnificent awareness of His infinite love and purpose.

The quarrel between science and religion is long-standing, but God will make use of the very tool—science—that has been used as justification for intellectual superiority to shun His truth and shut out His ultimate and absolute reality. In view of the vastness of the universe, we can see the minimization of man. By contrast, in view of the minuteness of the atom, we can see the magnification of God. Physicists have come to the conclusion that the atom is not the smallest particle, and that matter, as we know it, acts and reacts in ways that defy the laws of space and time. This leaves them scratching their highly intellectual heads and becoming more abstract in their musings than a small-town preacher. Could matter be spiritual? And spirit matter?

God's Spirit has shown me parallels between the physical world and the spiritual world. Whether or not these parallels are easily apparent is a matter of choice. We are the observers of reality as we choose to see it. Thanks to quantum physics, we can now recognize that there is another order of reality, one that lies beneath that which we have taken for granted for so long. This unseen realm seems to be built primarily on foundations of faith, but God's Spirit has given us many hints and suggestions in science. We just have to make a choice: We either choose to stay blind and refuse to *see* or we humbly admit that we are not our own gods.

It isn't a matter of what the world portrays to be the truth but what we *perceive* as the truth. The way we "see" things, people, and circumstances defines who we ultimately are in relationship to the world we live in. What we think and feel determines what we experience and perceive. However, there are many illusions out there ready to fool us. "We are born to inquire after Truth," Democritus said, but he never lived in a world like ours, where the truth hides behind virtual reality and digitally enhanced visual illusions. What chance do we have of discerning what is truly real if our eyes can lie to us and send incorrect messages to our brains? What a terrible and sad outcome awaits us then, unless there really is an absolute truth and reality.

There is—the I AM who transcends time and space and who never changes.

Reticular Activating System

The RAS is a bundle of nerves located at the base of the skull the size of a lima bean that filters our information pertinent to you. It works hand in hand with the "law of attraction".

You can activate your own RAS, which is the power you have to focus on what it is important to you. If God is the God of you and everything about you, by physiological nature then your brain will activate your RAS to see God everywhere around you.

Our God has created us to be creatures with a conscience, but we have the free will to activate it through the magnificent RAS in our brains.

The way I see it, the God-given reticular activating system works as the portal to our subconscious and deep into our souls to start seeing God's realm as the only genuine reality. It is about who we believe God is. And who—each one of us—have chosen to become in light of this divine knowledge.

Even if I don't see it, even if my logic says different, even if I have exhausted all other terms of understanding, I will keep moving because God has ordained me to do so. Two and a half years ago, all I had was random words with no correlation among them at all. All I knew was that they had something to do with "seeing."

The message is simple: GOD IS. And there is a reality far more real that what our senses can perceive. God's invitation for us to move from our reality to His has been extended from the time Jesus died on the cross.

He has been as patient and merciful as any father would be to his young child. But we are not that young and naïve anymore.

We have grown and ought to become more accountable for our actions. Our fear and pride have blinded us to spiritual truths all around us, and we hide behind cultural paradigms and scientific hopes to find measurable answers and especially behind religious superiority.

We are the church, the chosen people. Therefore, we should be the ones who lay down the bridge into God's kingdom. We ought to be the ones who humble ourselves and lay down our lives for our enemies.

Religion has failed history too many times. God's Spirit has shown me that using God's name in vain goes way beyond cursing. We use God's name in vain if we call ourselves Christians and yet hate or judge our brothers or deem them below our "spiritual pride."

There should be no "new Gentiles." God loves us all! Even us Christians. The approach we take toward God must be authentic as He is authentic. His Spirit is at work in all of us. Within each one of us. Individually. Now! Today!

Our accountability has grown parallel to the opportunities we now have to seek His will and pursue His mind. He is not elusive at all. He longs for us and craves our fellowship. We now have several ways to research the Bible and study it. So it is up to us. It comes down to our free will. We have a clear choice, and we no longer have an excuse not to make one.

A Dream

I have a dream.

I stand before a mirror and see my image reflected in it. Suddenly, I explode into millions of atoms and cells. Still conscious, I experience a sickening wave of panic and despair.

I need to have an image, a *shape*, in order to retain a sense of who I am.

There are mirrors all around me, showing reflections of images that are not my own. My dispersed atoms and cells visit each in turn, trying to conform myself to them while anxiety overwhelms me. I see images of other people; I try to form myself into their likeness, but I know it isn't working. I run to other mirrors, other reflections—images of material possessions and objects like cars, clothes, and boats. I try again to form myself into their likeness, but it only brings more pain to my broken image.

Finally, far in a corner, I see a mirror irradiating some kind of soft, soothing light. My disconnected and troubled atoms and cells rush to it and try to reform themselves into an image of what I see. From the moment I choose to do so, my consciousness experiences a sense of belonging. But it is not my own image that gives me this sense of peace and calm. I start to recognize Him as my wandering cells and atoms come together and begin to make sense of me. It is the image of God!

I know now that I am not the reality looking for an image. I am the reflection looking from the other side of the mirror for a reality!

I am not reality unless I choose to *be* the image of who *is* reality. I won't exist unless I choose to have an observer who looks over me.

Hidden From Our Eyes

> This is why I speak to them in parables: Though seeing, they do not see; though hearing, they do not hear or understand. In them is fulfilled the prophecy of Isaiah: "You will be ever hearing but never understanding; you will be ever seeing but never perceiving. For this people's heart has become calloused; they hardly hear with their ears, and they have closed their eyes. Otherwise they might see with their eyes, hear with their ears, understand with their hearts and turn, and I would heal them." (Matthew 13:13–15 NIV)

God's truth has been hidden in plain sight in His Word for those who seek to know Him. I've spent more than a year researching every appearance of the words *sight* and *eyes* in the Bible, and there is an awe-inspiring abundance of material. According to the New Testament, Jesus healed blind men in different ways. In one, He touched; in another, He forgave; and in yet another, He spat upon (Matthew 9:27–31; 12:22; 20:29–34; Mark 8:22–26; John 9:1–7). And yet we are still trying to put God in a box. We expect Him to do the things we want Him to do, the way we want Him to do them.

Do not trust what your physical eyes can see but seek the ultimate reality in Him. Rest assured, He *will* reveal Himself to you if you choose to seek Him, but you must seek Him with all your heart (Deuteronomy 4:29). He is the only reliable and absolute reality. He said he is "the I AM," everlasting present (Exodus 3:14; Isaiah 40:5).

For now, we should come to one conclusion: We are blind, and our lack of humility has twisted it all up from the beginning. We live within a crooked perception of reality and will not come to the awareness of this truth until we become purified children of God by humbly acknowledging that we are created beings (Philippians 2:15).

No Mumbo Jumbo

It is not my intent to convince you that this unseen spiritual realm may only be based upon a presumption of faith. As a matter of fact, God's Spirit has been teaching me what He really means by having faith in Him. Somehow, I had been under the impression that it did not matter whether I understood anything about God or not. It all was a matter of faith. A "just believe because I say so" kind of mentality.

This mind-set is the perfect breeding ground for whatever comes our way and leaves the door wide open for the opinions of others to become our own pseudo-beliefs. What my Bible says about faith differs from this way of thinking. "Now faith is being *sure* of what we hope for and *certain* of what we do not see" (Hebrews 11:1, emphasis added).

The words *sure* and *certain* do not quite agree with the mind-set of believing without proof, or concrete evidence. That is a "fluffy" kind of faith; the kind of faith that will easily fly from thought to thought, from feeling to feeling, but pop at the first sharp circumstance it encounters. I believe that true reality may be the total opposite (as in a mirror-like reflection) of what we have believed it to be.

It is more profitable, albeit erroneous, to believe we are our own gods, living on the other side of the mirror as if we were our own reality (2 Thessalonians 2:11; Isaiah 44:18; Ezekiel 12:2). But it is not lack of "eyes that see" that keeps us blind but rather our proud resolution of not humbling ourselves in front of Him. God reveals Himself to those who humble themselves and gives them insight into His kingdom. Humility allows us to tear off our cancerous pride and accept we have been created and are not our own (Colossians 1:16).

The divine paradox is brought into reality when we become aware that the instant we declare ourselves valueless, insignificant, and created, the power of the entire universe awakens in our dormant consciousness. We become aware of who we really are and who He really is because *we* have been created in **His** *image* (Genesis 1:27). Once our spiritual eyes finally open to this glorious truth, it is like taking off the cloak of darkness and lies and putting on a new nature, which allows us to finally see the ultimate and absolute reality (Ephesians 4:24).

God IS. We choose to be or not be. Without Him, we are like a shapeless bunch of cells and atoms, running from thing to thing, from thought to thought, from concept to concept, from virtual reality to virtual reality, trying to find our reflection in a mirror that makes sense. We have no hope of *being* unless we come to the realization that we are on the other side of the mirror (James 4:14; Psalm 39:6).

Time to See

"He says, 'Be still and know that I am God'" (Psalm 46:10).

Luckily, God has given us instructions on how to clear our vision. Let's take a closer look at the Bible verse above. "Be still [time standing still] and know [focus on the knowledge of Him] that I am God [experience Him]."

Knowing Him goes beyond just believing in Him. Believing *in* God is not as powerful as *believing* God. To *know* God is to have experienced Him in such a way that we become part of Him and He a part of us. God Himself has given us the capacity to grasp His magnificent wisdom. He yearns to have a close relationship with each one of us; an intimate relationship specifically catered to our own needs and personality.

I am evidence of such startling truth. He has chosen me—the most unlikely character—to distribute this message of awareness and reality. Perhaps it is because I am aware that life is full of distractions that try to blur the vision of His reality. And I have learned what it means to truly *see* Him. It comes down to a matter of personal choice. The continuous choices we make every single day ultimately define us. Our eyes will deceive us, our brain will lie to us, and the opinions of others will pull us to pieces. So what are we to do?

I can only tell you what I personally chose to do. I *chose* to believe that there is something much bigger than myself. I *chose* to believe that something or someone is the origin of everything that has ever been created, including myself. I *chose* to believe that His reality is not defined by this physical world and that His essence goes beyond what my eyes can see and my brain can comprehend. And the miracle is, He knows me and yearns to be known *by* me.

Seeing my son Casey's eyes starting to open is also gripping. He sent me the following letter not too long ago:

Sunny Day

by Casey Hopkins

When the sun rises and the clouds begin to glow, the warmness hits my skin, and I look out to the ocean; no land as far as the eye can see.
The horizon is but a thin line, separating one giant plane from another, but as the wind blows across my cheeks, I feel the exhilaration of being small. In this vast openness, I am so incredibly small that my conscious mind cannot fathom what my eyes see. What I *see* is not what I *feel*. I see the separation of sky and ocean, but I understand they are inseparable and to try to divide them is absurd. What I see is truth.

Truth is always relative to a point of view, and the appearance of the world is relative to our eyes, but what I see now is something that, even with alterations to the human sense of sight, I cannot find any word strong enough to express the beauty or perfection of the world around me. The world is an extension of myself, and I am wholly inseparable from it. My contribution is simply to acknowledge that what is, and that is it. I am what surrounds me and what surrounds me is myself; it has not become but always has been and anything in between shall come.
Standing here, I am with God, and there is love. Here is an emotional ecstasy of freedom and

purpose. When I feel the need to capture this moment to save it for a time of true despair, I cannot. And what a delight! I cannot stop the present, for it is. Obsessively, my mind wonders how this could be, wonders how to share the experience with someone else. Each thought passes by for only a moment; not in a rush, but leaving only to have fulfilled its purpose whether I understood it or not. If I did not understand, that was okay too. I do not feel any restriction in not knowing. The time will pass, and even if I was to never know anything again, that would be okay too.

To those who have seen what it is I've tried to describe, you know that we, you and I, have a relationship. The light from the sky reflects against the water and reflects against my soul. The water seems bluer on this day, and my soul explodes with more clarity and relief than thought possible. Being able to surrender thoughts of complexity was seamless with time. There is no future further than the present and the past is forever behind me. There is no climax of emotion that I must maintain because Earth is not the only thing my eyes are seeing. I am seeing the vastness of space and, ultimately, the greatness of God. I'm looking through the eyes God gave me, unobstructed by what man has made and understanding what God made. A thought occurs to me out of emptiness (or was it fullness?): " Why didn't God say what He made was great? This is surely better than good!"

And this is what the wind whispered to me, "God made man in His image so that you could see what He has made. Until this day, you have been blind." In this moment, I feel joy in knowing that I am not on the outside looking upon His creation in awe, but looking at it the way God had looked at it.

Anything that was myself was not mine, it was entwined with His, and what I held away from God to call my own, I freely gave away in fear that it was only a distraction from His true greatness. I have seen with my eyes what He created on the first day and how it has meaning. I do not try to control anything because there is nothing to control! It is all right in its place—myself not being master of it is exactly where I belong. That is to say, my sense of compassion has not been brought on by the self-absorption and righteousness that I had come to see. It is knowing that all that surrounds me has always been and encompasses me in a world where which things are such as they are. This day has had such an impact on me that I could write it a thousand times and never grasp the truest meaning of it all.

Casey wrote this heart filled letter while setting on the aircraft carrier George Washington of the U.S.A. Navy in Japan.

Our Choices

We are the sum total of our choices.

—Woody Allen

A strident characteristic of our human nature is that we do not like to give up our freedom of choice. We do not like to be told what to do or what to believe.

While we wake up to a clean slate of choices on a daily basis, we are also bound by the choices that have been made for us for the good of the community and culture we live in. We are faced with an endless array of seemingly "free" choices—the clothes we wear, what we eat for breakfast, the car we drive. But if we think about it, we know we are not free to go out without clothes, that whatever we eat for breakfast will have consequences to our health, and the car we drive is the car we could best afford. God's Spirit has shown me that the clusters of choices we perceive as "free" are nothing but an illusion.

It is *one* choice alone that heals our spiritual vision, and that is to acknowledge Him. This is the primary decision that will determine the essence of our existence on this earth and our destination once we pass through. He has given us enough contrast between good and evil, right and wrong, to make this decision easier. Not making a choice—not choosing to acknowledge Him—*is* a choice in and of itself.

Freedom and Paradox

The instant God elected to give us freedom of choice, He knew He was putting in our possession the very same characteristic that would make us more in His likeness. Philosopher Jean-Paul Sartre put it a bit more dramatically when he wrote, "We are condemned to be free." We either choose God or we do not. It is that one choice, hidden in the million illusionary ones, that makes us truly free. We are free to see things under the brilliance of His eternal, pure, and magnificent divine light or under the puny illumination of our own man-made wattage.

One choice: yes or no, on or off, light or darkness, life or death. The way I see it, if you do not choose one, you are choosing the other by default. There is no way out; you either choose God or you do not. That is the way it has been designed. Your complaints of unfairness or shrieks of "Foul!" are not going to change things. But the moment you do choose God, you are truly free. You can open the door to a life with real purpose under the spotlight of His incandescent splendor. In the very instant we recognize God as such, we open our eyes to His inconceivable reality and our own undiscovered and wonderful possibilities. We know then *why* we exist, and existence precedes essence. We take our first step into a startling and amazing journey of awareness; we become awake in the light of Yahweh!

One of the things made clear in this new light is the reconciliation of two seeming opposites, which I call the "divine paradox." I am in awe of the hundreds of paradoxes I see in my daily life when I pay attention. The Bible is full of them: You have to die in order to live, you have to give in order to receive, you have to be humble to experience glory, the way up is down, to be first you have to be the last, and so on, and so on. In the realm of His divine paradoxes, choice is elusive but very real. When we choose to see God, God gazes back into our eyes, once again giving us all the power over the universe that we had previously lost (Deuteronomy 30:20; 2 Peter 1:10).

God placed Adam in the garden of Eden and told him, "But of the tree of the knowledge of good and evil you shall not eat" (Genesis 2:17). He gave Adam a *choice*—to obey or disobey, to believe or disbelieve, to trust or distrust. Adam had been given the highest trait that made him more like God Himself—a free will, the power to choose. God gave us free will, and therefore He has no control over our individual power of choice. In this paradox lies the manifestation of His perfect and multidimensional love for us. However, God is God of all the rest. We are contained in space and time, over which He has total control. He only gave us freedom of choice—remember that. We have been purposely and intentionally made. But "made" nevertheless. So what keeps us from taking this first step of awareness? Why do we hesitate to choose His perfect light over our own imperfect illumination? This very idea of "being made," of being a creation, is what wounds our pride the most and keeps us from choosing to submit to the Creator of it all.

We have been trapped in a web of lies coming from all directions. They come from the world, from other people's opinions, from our culture and traditions, from false religions, from past experiences, and—most of all—from ourselves. Pride is only fear dressed up in layers of all these lies. We are afraid of what we do not understand but are too proud to admit it. Therefore, we just push it away and act as if we do not want it or even need it. Our fears are so devious and tend to hide so well that we become numb to them and, consequently, unaware of their presence. We become proud of being prideful (Obadiah 1:3).

Fear is defined as a distressing negative sensation induced by a perceived threat. First of all, it is a *sensation*, a feeling dictated by our brains—and by now I hope you have learned not to rely on the information your brain springs on you. Fear also leads us to *judge* whether something is good or bad, right or wrong. This is a cancerous concept that is deadly to our spiritual growth and lethal to His spiritual sight. Fear is at the core of the negative feelings that debilitate us.

But I believe it is the *object* of our fear that matters and makes a difference in the outcome. Do we fear the world? We will struggle with insecurity, yearning to be accepted at all costs. Do we fear the Lord? We will focus on that which pleases Him alone.

When physicists at first discovered black holes, they saw them as the end of everything—the disappearance of all matter to an infinite and unknown "nothingness." Nowadays, they have changed their minds and deem them to be not the endpoints but the beginning of everything.

The way I see it, God is trying to teach us a lesson. We should have learned by now that there is little out there—if anything—but God where we can safely place our faith. I have accepted the fact that I float on a pool of uncertainty with enough faith in my heart not to drown.

We all are participants in a God thought-play whereas on the atomic level—quantum mechanics level—atoms and electrons act in such a dazzling way that common sense explodes into a million pieces. Particles seem to appear and disappear at random. Nothing is certain, not even our own existence, unless there is an Observer.

If we were to hang this concept in front of the spiritual mirror, what would we see? The majority of physicists dream to not die before they "marry" the laws of the little (quantum mechanics) with the laws of the very big (law or relativity). In religion, we strive to unite the very small (humankind) with the very big (God).

Our flesh could simply ride through life without waking up to the spiritual connection with God, but we will never feel complete unless we become aware of His reality.

A Dream

I dream that God has placed me in the middle of the garden of Eden. I see two trees. I hear the voice of God. "You have access to all my creation, and you chose the Tree of Knowledge of Good and Evil."

I direct my attention to the Tree of Knowledge. It is startlingly divided in two. Half of it is pure white; the other half, pitch-black. I see people climbing up and down both sides of the tree, pulling each other from side to side. "*This* is the good side!" they scream as they tear each other apart. People on each side—light and dark—are convinced their side is the righteous side. And they are sure that those on the opposite side are evil.

From the moment when Adam and Eve chose to eat from the fruit of the Tree of Knowledge, we learned to judge for ourselves what and who is right and wrong. I immediately understand why it is that we deem ourselves to be more righteous than others—our spiritual eyes are shut.

God then points to the Tree of Life and says, "You had access to all of this, and you chose against it." This tree is wrapped up in light; it seems to be made of living fire. The bright light hurts my eyes, burns my corneas, blinds me to the physical world. I am free to see a new reality. I am free to see Him.

I draw closer to the tree, mesmerized and not at all worried about being right or wrong. I am just happy to *be*; to exist; to keep my eyes focused on the blinding light, which is slowly, carefully, and lovingly opening my spiritual eyes to the realm of His kingdom.

Adam and Eve's Choice

> Now the serpent was more crafty than any of the
> wild animals the LORD God had made. He said
> to the woman, "Did God really say, 'You must not
> eat from any tree in the garden'?" The woman said
> to the serpent, "We may eat fruit from the trees
> in the garden, but God did say, 'You must not eat
> fruit from the tree that is in the middle of the
> garden, and you must not touch it, or you will die.'
> " "You will not surely die," the serpent said to the
> woman. "For God knows that when you eat of it
> your eyes will be opened, and you will be like God,
> knowing good and evil." (Genesis 3:1–5)

"Your eyes will be opened"—there lays the lie! Our eyes are
closed. "And you will know good and evil"—another lie! It is only
God who judges, who is allowed to pronounce what is right and
what is wrong. We only make a mess out of the world when we
try to judge others. People have killed each other for centuries
over warring ideas of whose beliefs are correct, whose religion
is better than the other's.

> When the woman saw that the fruit of the tree
> was good for food and pleasing to the eye, and
> also desirable for gaining wisdom, she took some
> and ate it. She also gave some to her husband, who
> was with her, and he ate it. Then the eyes of both
> of them were opened, and they realized they were
> naked; so they sewed fig leaves together and made
> coverings for themselves. (Genesis 3:7–8)

Do you see?

Immediately after Eve bit into the lie, she "saw that the fruit of the tree was good for food and pleasing to the eye." She *saw* for the first time using only her *physical* eyes. Adam and Eve lost the ability to see with the *spiritual* eyes God had initially given them. Their spiritual perception became distorted and blurry. By choosing to eat from the Tree of Knowledge, they dimmed the incandescent light of God and began to see the world through their own imperfect illumination; the physical illumination that showed them their nakedness and introduced shame into the human condition.

The bad news is that, because of this, we are all born spiritually blind. The choice Adam and Eve made has blocked the clarity of God's light and has hampered our spiritual vision. The good news is that we can all learn to see again. When we approach the great choice with humility, the light of God can destroy our physical eyes and make our spiritual eyes new again.

It is all about what we choose to believe in, how we choose to act, and what we choose to do with this new revelation. And we are not to be distracted—we must stay focused on that light. My eyes are only on Him—nothing else, no one else. I am not to compare myself to others, for I am no better or no worse than anyone else. I am not to worry about anyone's faults but my own. Once I accept that I am His creation, and His light has sharpened my spiritual vision, I must let Him shape me. I must have faith to become the perfect tool for His divine purpose of service to others.

Faith

So what is faith? Is faith blind? Or is faith actually able to see beyond our present circumstances? I think faith is being conscious and able to see what no one else can see—that which is withheld from our physical eyes but reveals itself, crystal clear, to our spiritual eyes in the light of God's reality. Faith believes in what it knows to be real. But I think there is something dangerously wrong with our faith nowadays.

We profess to have "blind faith" with our lips, but it never touches our heart. The only thing we have learned is to repeat empty words and platitudes we have heard our entire lives. Faith is stringently connected with obedience and trust—and godly humility. It takes godly humility to *move* in obedience by faith. The word *move* is important. God often asks us to journey beyond what we humanly perceive as reality and goads us to act against our own individual logic (Luke 5:5). We react—He acts. We move—He moves. His movement, incidentally, is constant and persistent. His Spirit is forever in perpetual motion.

The Tree

A couple of weeks ago, I sat beside a majestic oak tree by a church close to my house. I was hoping to capture the maze of its branches and the texture of its massive trunk in a painting. After twenty minutes of staring at it, all I could think of was how lucky I was that my eyes could witness such beauty. Just two days later, a storm came and knocked the mighty tree down, right in front of the church's door. I was appalled. I felt the need to see it with my own eyes; when I did, the tears rushed out in disbelief. I was probably the last human on Earth to have feasted on its magnificence, and the thought saddened me.

There was a gentlemen cutting up the huge trunk and winding branches, and as he cleared away the mess, he tried to comfort me. "Don't cry for this big ol' tree, sweetie," he said. "Cry for those who do not have Christ in their lives." He explained that the congregation had known that this tree was rotten inside. It had long been weakened by bugs and termites, and they had been afraid that one day it was going to fall right on top of their little church and cause great damage.

I did not believe it was only a coincidence that it grew right beside a church. And it was definitely not just any "ol' tree." It was considered the oldest burn oak tree in the state of Tennessee. Many professional photographers and painters had lingered under its glorious shadows and admired its beauty. I turned my eyes to God and begged Him to explain the spiritual reality being revealed to me through such circumstances. I woke up the next day with the answer. That once-mighty tree, now rotten and fallen, was the perfect picture of our empty faith.

How many of us have that kind of faith? Standing proud with arms stretched out as if to say, "Look at my strong faith. Come and sit under my shadow, and let me pray for you." And then, out of nowhere, a storm hits our lives, and our faith is knocked down to the ground, our illusory strength nothing more than tangled branches and scrap wood. Faith is tested by raw circumstances. Our reaction in the face of harsh circumstances is where real faith shines. Anything that crumbles in the presence of trouble is only a shadow, an illusion of faith. Perseverance and steadfastness are the very traits of real faith. And faith, in turn, feeds on them both (Luke 8:25).

Instead of trying to impress those around us with our faith by our works and words, we ought to marvel God with our faith in what *He* can do.

Our Reality

Reality is merely an illusion, albeit a very persistent one.

—Albert Einstein

*O*ur subjective reality—what we see—is really only a reflection of what is certainly and absolutely *real*. We buy the illusion, and doing so has blinded our spiritual eyes and blocked us from God's light. Living in this distorted reality has given rise to fear, anxiety, and guilt, all of which have putrefied our minds. But a higher level of consciousness brings about the awareness of the freedom we innately possess as created beings of God—the freedom to choose. Once we have made the first, imperative choice to believe in an absolute creating Power, we begin to see through the ephemeral nature of our own reality. We begin to glimpse the patterns that will define the complex relationship between God, the rest of mankind, and ourselves.

I've been working hard to identify and remove the factors that have blurred my spiritual vision for so many years. I have tried to rid myself of preconceived ideas and systems of thinking, and this has opened a portal to a new dimension of universal and godly vision that I now know has from the beginning rested on my God-given choice. Until two years ago, I was strolling through life with the false notion I was not blind. But if quantum physics has validated anything, it is the realization that absolutely nothing exists as we *see* it. There is a reality beyond our senses and beyond our sense of self.

Quantum physics states that the universe is made of energy, space, mass, and time, all interpenetrating each other. This cosmic jumble would be terrifying if I looked at it in the warped reflection of my own false reality. Fortunately, I don't have to. God has given me grace in the shape of a spiritual mirror that I can place in front of any given physical reality in order to see the greater spiritual truth. God can make one of many and many of one. He *created* energy, space, mass, and time. And He has enabled me to become aware of His kingdom; to choose to see my life reflected in His reality rather than my own.

The Magic Bullet?

The majority of theoretical physicists are very spiritual. I guess they can't help it in view of what they experience in their field. I'm sure many of them would like to put a stop to the wild notion that science has all the answers. They know better than anyone that science has only opened the door to more unanswered questions. Physicists are eyewitnesses to the myriad of unexplained phenomena that do not quite square with their equations and find themselves wondering where the laws of physics come from in the first place. Who set these laws into motion? And why doesn't the law of the "big" align with the law of the "small"? Physicists are more aware than most that what we call reality is a big illusion.

The close observation of physical realities can open our spiritual eyes. It can show us spiritual realities that parallel paradoxes found in the physical world. Nonetheless, there are some in the scientific community who are trigger-happy and eager to shoot, hoping to kill religion once and for all. I can't say I blame them. In fact, I think God is very tempted to let them have the bullets. Religion is not exactly what God intended either. It is part of the reason we are blind to His reality.

"For Christ did not enter a man-made sanctuary that was only a copy of the true one; he entered heaven itself, now to appear for us in God's presence" (Hebrews 9:24). God's reality manifested itself in the body of Jesus Christ. And that reality did not reveal itself in the "man-made" place of worship. His reality cannot be contained within the hard-and-fast rules of a denominational dogma or a strict scientific theorem. Those who believe firmly in their preconceived notions—religious *or* scientific—need to borrow a page from the book of theoretical physics. We cannot choose to live within His reality if we are too attached to our own.

Let the Cat Make a Choice

In 1935, Erwin Schrödinger came up with a rather cruel thought experiment. In a hypothetical scenario, he placed a virtual cat inside a box to provoke thought and discussion as to the probabilities of the cat being dead or alive, without the dispensation of actually observing it. The scenario is this: A cat is placed into a steel chamber, along with a device containing a vial of hydrocyanic acid, a radioactive substance. If even a single atom of the substance decays during the test period, a relay mechanism will trip a hammer, which will, in turn, break the vial and kill the cat.

Since from outside the steel chamber we cannot know whether or not an atom of the substance has decayed—and, consequently, cannot know whether the vial has been broken, the hydrocyanic acid released, and the cat killed—according to quantum law, the cat is both dead *and* alive in what is called a superposition of states.

I see this as just another example of a divine paradox; a perfect opportunity to put a physical circumstance (even if it is speculative) in front of the spiritual mirror. In our lives, we are, like Schrödinger's imaginary feline, both dead and alive. In one universe, the cat is dead. That is like being in our distorted reality without God (Ephesians 2:1). But we have a choice. There is another universe, one in which the cat is alive. When we let go of our own notions of reality, we can live in Christ (Ephesians 2:4–5). According to quantum mechanics, reality is only real if there is an observer. God is our ultimate observer. God sees (Genesis 16:13).

A Thrilling Ride

My husband and I went to Universal Studios a few months ago. It's been a while since I've been there, and I was stunned at the way reality was intertwined so seamlessly with fiction. There were moments I had to stop and actually touch the trees or plants around me to see if they were real or not.

The rides were even more astonishingly realistic than the landscape. Before I got on the "Harry Potter and the Forbidden Journey " ride, I gave myself a little reality check and remembered that whatever I was about to experience was not going to be real.

Despite what my eyes might see or my body might feel in being rushed into the air, it was not actually occurring. I wasn't going to be able to trust the evidence of my own senses in there.

But even with this little pep talk lingering in my mind, it was hard to believe that what I was seeing wasn't real. When the car took off, Harry Potter showed up in front of me in 3D, and the machinery started to shake my whole body. It seemed so real that I became sick to my stomach. I had to close my eyes for an instant and tell myself once again that what I was experiencing was not actually happening. I had to remind myself it was only an amusement park ride, built with the intention of entertaining me and helping me to have some fun! And fun I was about to have! I opened my eyes. I was flying right behind Harry and Ron, evading evil ghosts and dodging the balls of fire they threw at us.

As I got off the ride—feeling heroic for defeating the enemy and wearing a big smile on my face—God took the opportunity to share a beautiful insight. "Remember, life was meant to be good. Life is meant to be a thrilling ride, full of adventures and wonderful journeys." And it is, once you acknowledge the One who is behind it all. The One who put the ride together and is behind the controls. And when you acknowledge that which is real, He is the One who has the power to turn everything on or off. I'm only here to experience it. Fortunately, the One behind all the controls is someone who loves me dearly, and His only desire is my acknowledgment. Whatever comes my way in the form of tribulations or problems are not as real as the lesson to be learned and the ultimate gain in the development of my spiritual growth. God is always behind the controls.

However, I still have a choice. I choose the attitude with which I view the ride. I can get on the ride of life either foolishly believing I am in control or I can humble myself and acknowledge that I am not. I choose to jump wholeheartedly into the car, buckle myself in, and be thankful that this ride of life is going to bring me back to the One who initiated it all.

A Dream

I have a dream.

I'm in a hallway filled with mirrors—a funhouse of some sort, the kind you find at a fair. Each mirror is a different shape, and I run from mirror to mirror, delighting in watching my reflection. It becomes distorted and warped differently in each mirror, the shape of the frame dictating my perception.

But then it comes to me—there's a spiritual lesson here. I can *choose* which mirror to stand in front of. It is not that there are many realities out there. There is only *one* absolute reality, but we get to choose our perception of it.

I can see myself in a distorted reflection and choose to believe that is who I really am. Or I can choose to see myself in the reflection of God's reality—the way I'm meant to be.

Perception

> Do not conform any longer to the pattern of this world, but be transformed by the renewing of your mind. Then you will be able to test and approve what God's will is—His good, pleasing, and perfect will. (Romans 12:2)

It is more about perception than sight. The object we are looking at never changes, but our perception of it does. We can look at the world and all the people, circumstances, joys, and troubles it contains through different lenses. The "pattern of this world" is our distorted reality. But when we renew our mind, we can see through the lens of God's reality. We will have a distorted perception of reality until we see ourselves as the reflection of the perfect I Am.

Our reality is real only if we choose to reflect Him. Another divine paradox! This concept is so clear to the spiritual eyes and yet so difficult to the natural human mind.

God is communicating with us now like Jesus did two thousand years ago. Jesus captured his audience by presenting a clear vision of the kingdom of God in terms and images they could easily relate to and understand. God, using me, His lowly servant, is letting His light shine that much brighter against the backdrop of my inabilities. I am evidence that you do not need to be a highly intellectual individual to pierce our false reality. You only need to choose to want to (Proverbs 2:3–5). Our reality intermingles with our choice to the point that it can either reconcile us with God for all eternity or separate us from Him forever.

For us to attempt to understand God matters, we have to let our minds and spirit flow at the rhythm of His breath, in and out.

Our minds still want to separate things, judge good from evil, right from wrong, and categorize, label, and compartmentalize them accordingly ... as if we were gods.

Jesus told His disciples that His kingdom was a present reality (Matthew 12:28; 13:18–23; 21:43), and then he also said it was a hope for the future (Matthew 16:28; 20:20–23; 26:9). So was He contradicting Himself? When is it then? Is His kingdom now or for the future?

The way I see it is that, again, time does not play by the rules in His kingdom. Perhaps like the particles in quantum physics become "real" when they are observed, we become real citizens of the real kingdom when we allow ourselves to be observed by the heavenly Observer and Participator!

"Though seeing, they do not see; though hearing, they do not hear or understand" (Matthew 13:10–13). We have to keep in mind our visual perception of spiritual matters may become divine paradoxes as optical illusions that obscure our understanding and logic. Open your spiritual eyes and SEE! "Ephphatha!" (Mark 7:34).

Changing Our Reality

Since we are spiritually blind, it is easy for us to accept that the spiritual realm is more of an abstract reality than the physical world we know and experience through our senses. But in fact, God's reality is *far* more real than our own. He is the only reality. He who calls himself the I AM.

When we decide to operate under His holy light, we are no longer blind. Our spiritual eyes are wide open, and we finally see the connection between God and each one of us. Our brain is then able to shift into a state of greater capacity, to go beyond our five senses and begin to understand the spiritual realities all around us. We seek understanding, we look around, and then we make a choice. Do we choose our own reality—a distorted place of scientific half-truths and theological turmoil? Or do we look beyond to His ultimate, true reality? To the way His world is meant to be? I made my choice, and He said,

> I love you more than those who say you are nothing but a result of a chaotic bang from a mud puddle.

> I love you more than those who say they know who is righteous and who is sinful.

> I love you more than those who say your ancestors were hairy monkeys on the trees.

> I love you more than those who say you are doomed to live a life without a purpose and to die without hope.

> I love you more than those who hope to attain their salvation through good works and perfect church attendance.

> I love you so much that I have given you the God-like characteristic that will either pull you away from or bring you closer to Me.

> I love you so much that I created you in My image so you will never be lost in ambiguity and will find yourself when you find Me.

I love you so much that I gave you the freedom to love Me back in response to my ultimate sacrifice for you—My son, Jesus Christ.

I love you so much I gave you the spiritual vision to see Me watching over you.

This is reality! This is the true nature of life, the universe, everything!

The choice is ours. God is offering us an escape from our imperfect and illusive realm. We just have to choose to take it. When we open the door to His kingdom with the key of humility, we are given access to His eyes, we are made aware of His choice, and we can enter into His reality.

Humility:
The Key to His Kingdom

Do you wish to rise? Begin by descending. You plan a tower that will pierce the clouds? Lay first the foundation of humility.

—Saint Augustine

As we've discussed before, we are all born spiritually blind. Because of that first, ultimate choice made long ago by Adam and Eve, we came into the world with eyes unable to see God's reality, unable to process His divine light. But we are somehow subtly aware of the existence of another, truer realm; even though we cannot see it, our consciousness can become cognizant of this place, these spiritual stimuli that affect our decisions and behaviors. As we grow in this understanding, we are told there is hope of a clearer vision. We realize there is a light far greater than that used here on Earth. And we are presented with a choice. Do we accept that we are blind and need help? Or are we plenty comfortable with the way things are? Do we enjoy the spiritual equivalent of the fashion eyeglasses and sunglasses that display our acquisitive power to the world?

The paths and systems humanity has created to navigate around our spiritual blindness keep us feeling safe, at least for a time. But then we encounter a big bump in the road or maybe someone we know has fallen off the cliff. Then we start thinking that maybe there is more to this. Maybe we're not seeing things clearly, as they really are, despite our impressive array of expensive eyewear.

The choice is ours. And it is an individual choice. Our sense of vision—be it spiritual or worldly—is always unique. God made us individuals, and He sees us *as* individuals. Like an optometrist fiddling with prescriptions, the lenses necessary to sharpen our spiritual vision are different for every one of us. But it does require abundant, total *humility* to accept that we cannot see this reality with our mortal eyes, and that acceptance is the first step toward clearer vision. Humility is the key to His eyes, His reality—His kingdom.

The Natural Man

The "natural man" is the one who says in his heart that there is no God. He believes himself self-sufficient; he does not crave an explanation of where he comes from or where he will go after he dies. *This is it*, he thinks and accepts the cards he has been dealt in life. (1 Cor. 2:14)

He relies on the knowledge acquired by his own studies and recollected facts and opinions of others, which he has deemed as accurate and acceptable. He trusts his own abilities to handle all matters of life. His beginning and end are quite short. He is born one day and on another he dies. When he faces trouble, he has nowhere else to go but to his small spectrum of human resources. He requires all questions to be answered in a logical, structured, sensible, and scientific form. His pride is usually his intellect. He compulsively compares himself to his peers in search of self-value. He is limited by his own understanding of self, empowered by the riches of his own pride, blinded by the sight of his own image. In other words, he is *us* before we come to realize our spiritual blindness. He is *us* before we realize we are not our own. He is what we are if we let ourselves be led astray by pride.

The Emperor's Clothes

"All of you clothe yourselves with humility toward one another, because, 'God opposes the proud but gives grace to the humble'" (1 Peter 5:5).

The Spirit's diligent job has been to teach me about humility for years now. I still do not completely grasp it, I admit, but I've learned enough to know that it is the main ingredient for the recipe of salvation.

He woke me up one day and told me, "I have dressed you with humility when I found you naked with pride." Then He reminded me of the fairy tale, "The Emperor's New Clothes." In case you missed it in your childhood, the story tells about how a very proud and foolish king was duped by two tailors who promised him a suit of the richest, finest fabric with a very special property—it couldn't be seen by those who were unworthy of his high rank. The king, of course, sees nothing when he looks into the mirror but his own birthday suit, but he pretends he can to assuage his sense of pride, which is so great that he steps out of his castle in the invisible suit for a procession among his subjects. Since his subjects have also heard about this rich, magical fabric, their own pride compels them to play along, pretending to be impressed by the fineness of the clothing. There is only a single a child—too innocent and young to understand the prideful reasons for the deception—who speaks up and points out that the prideful king is, in fact, naked.

I know for a fact that there are millions of people dressed up in their invisible pride. The "natural man" is one. And they refuse to become aware of it because of the very same pride. They do not want to see the nakedness of their humility. When you clothe yourself in godly humility, you see nothing in the mirror but your own faults being vanquished by the overpowering Spirit of God.

I had it so wrong about humility. I thought it meant walking around with my head down, feeling small and unworthy. Then He showed me that humility was more like walking with my hands up with my eyes on Him alone—*knowing* that I am unworthy.

To humble yourself is really just to fall in love with God. To love Him more than your own life and give it all up for Him. To exchange yourself for Him. To give up your dreams and thoughts and consider everything of lesser importance than Him. To be willing to lose your mind in exchange for His. Look up the word *fall* in the dictionary, and you will see definitions similar to those of the word *humility*: to drop one self to a lower position, to become lower in degree, to decline in quality, and so on. Let yourself fall in love; let yourself be humble. He is faithful and will catch you and gently pull you up to His own heart.

When His Spirit started to reveal Himself so strongly in my life, I decided to be humble and keep it to myself. I didn't want anyone to think that I thought too highly of myself because

God was speaking to me (1 John 2:27). Then I realized that what I was really afraid of was what people would think of me. I wasn't being humble; I was afraid I would be scrutinized and rejected. The acceptance of others had become more important than my obedience and submission to God. The only way to avoid this false humility is obedience and seeking out His will like a hidden treasure. Divine paradox ordains that godliness can only be understood by the simple and humble in heart (1 Corinthians 2:9–16).

"One's pride will bring him low, but he who is lowly in spirit will obtain honor" (Proverbs 29:3). Godly humility is something that it is hard for our human mind to even comprehend. It is another beautiful divine paradox—to gain honor in humility. I imagine bowing down in humility, closing my eyes in submission, and opening my arms in surrender to fly! When we trade in our pride for humility, when we acknowledge ourselves as His creations, we are finally able to make the one choice that really matters. We are able to seek His kingdom.

A Dream

I have a dream.

I see people falling into a dark, gaping maw. A black hole. They're being pulled by an overwhelming gravitational force, which God's Spirit told me was sin.

The people are falling, struggling, into this sin pit; caught up in a vortex of darkness and lies. No matter how hard they struggle, no matter how hard they fight the gravitational pull, they inevitably topple into the ominous whirl before disappearing, forever, into the frightening black hole at the bottom.

Suddenly, I hear a loud snapping sound. It is a rather pleasant sound; a sound of liberation, like iron shackles breaking and falling to the ground. Some people had made the right choice. They were acknowledging God and His Son, Jesus Christ. They stopped struggling in darkness and gave themselves in total humility to God's hands. He snatched them away from the terrible pull, breaking forever the bonds of sin and empowering us to resist it.

When sin entered the world, a spiritual black hole was formed, and we were all pulled into it. But we were also given a choice to say yes to God, His Son, and the Holy Spirit, which sets us free.

A Conversation with God

Humility has helped me to see that there is nothing I own and nothing in my life worth more than my relationship with God. That was a hard lesson for me to learn. When God's Spirit asked me to dispossess myself of everything I owned, the conversation followed this course:

Spirit of God: What if you lose your house and all your possessions? Would you still trust Me?

Me: I'd still love You, Lord, and I know You will provide.

Spirit of God: What if you lose your family, your friends, your husband? Will you still worship Me?

Me: Well, Father, that would definitely be much harder, but I would trust You, Lord, and give them all back to You.

Spirit of God: What about your children? Would you sacrifice them for My glory?

Me: Oh no, Lord! Please don't. I cannot bear the thought of losing my children. I cannot do that!

I played it over and over in my mind. I was able to strip myself of everything but my children. That was a step I could not take. Three years later, God's Spirit asked me again, "Are you ready to give up your children for My sake?"

I was driving and had to pull over because tears suddenly filled my eyes. I felt like my heart was being pulled out of my chest when I finally said, "Yes, Lord, I give my children back to You."

I remember the breathless, helpless feeling I had when I knew in my heart I had no idea of the fate God had for my children. But I had to humble myself and hold onto the belief that God is God, and that He was a better guardian of my children's future than I was. He grew me much, much smaller that day.

"String" Theory

It's hard to give up what we see as our control of our own fate. God's Spirit reminded me of another favorite childhood story— Pinocchio. Papa Gepetto carved Pinocchio from the trunk of a tree. There was no value in the wood itself but rather in the heart he put in it. He crafted Pinocchio in his image. When Papa Gepetto gave Pinocchio life, he also gave him the freedom to leave his house in search of education and self-growth. But Pinocchio was not particularly interested in what he could make of himself. All he could think about was what he did *not* want to be. He did not want to be a wooden puppet, a created being. He wanted to be a "real" boy. He wanted to pretend he had no strings attached. So, full of pride, he went out looking for adventure instead of education and was soon caught by someone who made a puppet out of him. He ran smack into the exact fate he was trying to avoid.

Papa Gepetto went out to find his wooden boy, was caught in a storm, and was swallowed by a giant whale, where he stayed three days. (Interesting, isn't it? Maybe the writer of this story did have a hidden agenda. When I researched it, I was amused by the fact that *Pinocchio* means "eye of wood.") But Gepetto was eventually reunited with his creation. And once Pinocchio had the humility to realize that the love of his father was more important than his own autonomy, he became "real."

I like to think of God as the Papa Gepetto to our Pinocchio. I come from dirt. I would not have value were it not for the love of the Father who chose to craft me into being and created me in His image. I choose to dwell in His house and humbly offer Him all my strings.

> Take them all, Lord.
> Take my dreams and my fears.
> Take my smile and my tears.
> Every string of my being
> I offer back to You,
> Whom now my eyes are seeing.
> Take them all, Father.
> Take my heart and my mind.
> Take my hands and my eyes.
> I know You will forever be kind.
> With every cell of my being,
> Hold onto my past and my future
> Like twines in Your holy hands,
> And holding hands with my feet on top of yours,
> Let's together dance!

I have freely given God my all and, in return, He has given me the key to His kingdom. I do not pretend to be anything I am not—I'm only a puppet—but the Master of the universe knows me by name. He is the God of all, and He is calling your name too.

Turning the Key

The way I see it, we keep the door closed by our own choice to keep it locked with pride.

Pride has many faces and the most dangerous one is the one that looks like "human humility", which God's spirit has taught me is so different than "Godly humility". We must humble ourselves before Him and get rid of any spiritual pride that may be clouding our spiritual sight.

We must stop foolishly fighting our own battles, struggling against a fate too dark and powerful for us to conquer. When we give it all to God, in absolute godly humility, He will save us. He will protect us. And He will usher us into His kingdom.

His Eyes

The only thing worse than being blind is having sight but no vision.

—Helen Keller

See

See is the last word in my journal entry on 10/21/09. It's in all capitals, at the bottom of the page, right in the middle of the line. I was begging God one more time not to give up on me.

> *I do not understand it all, I sense something going on in my life. A change. There is something ready to happen. I do not know what, but my life is taking a turn. A sharp corner, a stretch, something ...*
>
> *I sense God is trying to purify me. And still, I'm so confused. Things and thoughts move randomly in my head. Can't concentrate, can't focus, don't have a direction. Too many thoughts at the same time, and then nothing. Quietness. I only pray I won't miss the boat, that I may not see the light or miss the jump.*

God, please do not leave it up to me. I am not able. Carry me. I do want to do Your will above everything else, but do place me right under it, right in it.

I give up all my choices. I surrender all. I don't have much to offer but an empty vessel. I want to be all these things and still do not reach the surface of the necessary talent or ability.

God is taking me through a purifying process and is stripping me of my junk-self. Shining His light in dark crevices and cleaning house.

I am so slow, Lord. Do not let me miss Your will. I want to hear Your voice even more clear so I won't stray. Look at my heart.

SEE.

I've started this book in my head so many times for so long, and it always ends up staying there—in my head. I've argued with the Spirit of God for years. The day I wrote that journal entry was not the first time I was begging God to not give up on me, begging him to *see* my willing heart in spite of my inadequacies.

The very next day, on Thursday, October 22, 2009 at 11:08 a.m., my sister-in-law Joni sent me this e-mail:

Grace,
For some reason, you have been in my spirit the past two days?? Just know I am praying for you and I love ya so!!!!!!!!!!!

God says to tell you He has everything under control and "He sees"?? Not sure what that means, but He does, and maybe you do or will!!
Love, your Sis

The hair on the back of my neck stood up as I read that e-mail. I stared at the computer screen in disbelief and almost looked over my shoulder to see if He was really there, watching me. But I could not move. I was afraid. Isn't that always the way it is? Everyday, we pray to God for miracles and say we believe in His faithfulness to answer our prayers. But if we face Him in our own "reality"—when He's right there in front of us, on the screen of our laptops—we freeze! I mean, He can't be *that* real, can He? Yes, He can! And this book proves it. I am evidence of His power. I am Exhibit "A."

Right after that e-mail, things started happening in my life. An explosion of "coincidences" took over my daily existence, and my life stopped being lived by only me. Now there was a higher power living it for me—showing me where to go, whom to meet, what book to read. I had always known that God talked to me. But now I was hearing Him *sing*. I heard His music and His melody, and I learned to sway to His music. And as He sings to me, I am getting a clearer vision of His true reality. I'm learning to not only hear Him but to *see* Him too.

El-Roi

"She gave this name to the LORD who spoke to her: 'You are the God who sees me,' for she said, 'I have now seen the One who sees me' " (Genesis 16:13).

"The God of my vision." That is the name Hagar gave Jehovah when she encountered Him in the desert after being rejected by Sarai and Abram. To see God and live was contrary to expectation. Who she saw was who had been looking at her through all her trials. There is comfort in knowing that our loving Father's eyes are fixed on us.

If you have raised children, you'll know that their favorite phrase is often, "Look, Mommy, look!!" We are the same with our Lord God. We crave his attention; we long to have his eyes upon us. His loving gaze, full of grace and mercy, helps us recognize His omnipresence and omniscience. He truly is the God who *sees all things.* He sees our hearts. We cannot hide from Him.

It is not about me but about what His power can do through me (1 Corinthians 2:1–5). That was one of the things He wanted me to see—that He is seeing me at all times—and He wanted me to see Him back. I am watching Him watch me (Psalm 33:18; Psalm 34:15; Proverbs 15:3).

Awareness

How, then, can we become aware? How can we learn to see the eyes of God watching over us? The way I see it, since we are born spiritually blind, it is impossible to become aware without divine intervention. But I believe the eyes of God never move away from His creation. He is a permanent, constant, omnipresent consciousness of absolute love hovering over us freely, giving us the ability to perceive and become conscious of our own existence. The very fact nobody has been able to pin down the definition and entire understanding of our "consciousness" leads me to believe that it must be of divine order.

All human beings experience this consciousness at different levels of awareness. There are millions of people living life as it comes, never becoming aware of the meaning of life itself. They see the world around them with their physical eyes, unaware of the beatific gaze of God. It is only when we choose to humble ourselves and accept our insignificance that our spiritual sight is restored; it is this sight that frees our spirit to a higher state of consciousness and awareness. This is one of the lessons God is trying to teach us—to become *aware* of our reality. To become aware that we are blind, that we do not really see. When we accept this, we become awake to His reality, in awe of Yahweh (Matthew 5:8).

Our world craves awareness. There are so many groups dedicated to raising awareness of situations that may otherwise go unnoticed: cancer awareness, autism awareness, animal control awareness ... the list goes on and on. But I've never seen a 5k marathon, a plastic bracelet, or a t-shirt trying to get the word out about *spiritual* awareness. We desperately need it. We are not aware enough to *see* God, and we don't know how to even describe this lack of awareness. As soon as the word *God* is brought up in conversation, we slip into hiding behind our self-imposed and preconceived ideas of faith and religion.

Since He is the source of consciousness, being absolute consciousness Himself, we cannot draw conscious awareness unless we draw it from the source. Yet we cannot experience awareness—Absolute Consciousness—unless we choose to become observant and focused. The knowledge of God Himself has not been denied to us. It's only been hidden.

Even If

When we become aware of His presence—transcending our own understanding and sight—we learn to live by the "even if."

To live by the "even if" is to trust God so completely your mind is already made up in advance. Decisions have been made long before the manifestation of the final outcome. "Even if" is winning the battle in your mind before you actually enter the fray. It is making an eternal choice to believe and trust in God, whatever circumstance may come to you. It is having a total disregard of the outcome because you have absolute confidence that God never loses control.

"Even if" is taking our eyes out and offering them to Him; it is entrusting Him with our spiritual sight. It is being willing to lose our mind in exchange for gaining His (1 Corinthians 2:16). It is building the trench before the battle, building the shelter before the storm, having enough capital in your faith bank that you'll never go broke. To live by the "even if" is to count the cost and be willing to pay for it, in full. It is learning to walk in the dark with total assurance that the voice you hear will safely guide you through minefields.

Living by the "even if" means letting go of your fears and learning to live by "heartsight" rather than by eyesight. It is trusting God and keeping your eyes on Him as you move toward your uncertainties.

There are countless biblical examples of those who embraced the "even if" worldview. Moses (Exodus 4:1–24), Abraham (Genesis 22:11–19), Daniel (Daniel 3:16–18), Job (Job 13:15), Paul (Acts 20:24; Romans 8:28, 37; 1 Corinthians 15:58), and Peter (Matthew 26:35) are among them.

"Even if" implies perpetual and everlasting VICTORY!

A Dream

I have a dream.

I am looking straight in front of me. It takes me a moment to realize that I am completely unable to see.

As I become aware of my blindness, I wonder what I should do. I feel powerless and frightened. But the Spirit of God speaks to me and gives me guidance.

By choice, I pull my physical eyes out of their sockets and offer them up to God. In exchange, He lets His light in. It courses throughout my entire body, filling it with divine brilliance. His light fills the empty sockets my earthly eyes left behind. I can finally *see* Him in all His glory and majesty.

"Heartsight"

We are to see beyond what our eyes can see. We are to understand beyond the capacities of our brains. In order to gain awareness and see His benevolent gaze, we have to open the eyes of our heart (Ephesians 1:18). There are many instances in the New Testament where Jesus heals both the physically blind and the spiritually blind. In the Old Testament, we can see where God opened the eyes of the servant in order to assuage his fears and assure him that He's got it all under control:

> Then he sent horses and chariots and a strong force there. They went by night and surrounded the city. When the servant of the man of God got up and went out early the next morning, an army with horses and chariots had surrounded the city. "Oh, my lord, what shall we do?" the servant asked. "Don't be afraid," the prophet answered. "Those who are with us are more than those who are with them." And Elisha prayed, "O LORD, open his eyes so he may see." Then the LORD opened the servant's eyes, and he looked and saw the hills full of horses and chariots of fire all around Elisha. (2 Kings 6:14–17)

Do you see? When the Lord opened the servant's spiritual eyes, he could see proof of God's presence; a divine army signifying the love and protection available to those who are in relationship with God. His *eye*sight only showed him the number of the enemies arrayed against them. But his *heart*sight saw the truer reality. Our eyes are not reliable conductors of true information. Our brains are not designed to capture the knowledge of God. Our spiritual eyes can see God's reality; our spirit that is able to connect to God's Spirit. Once our spiritual eyes are opened, we can see His reality, where we are conquerors, victorious and unafraid. "I pray also that the eyes of your heart may be enlightened in order that you may know the hope to which he has called you, the riches of his glorious inheritance in the saints" (Ephesians 1:18).

Now I See

The glories of the Lord did not stop with Elisha's chariots of fire or even with Jesus' healing ministry in the New Testament. Miracles still occur in the modern world. God has shown me that He can heal both spiritual and physical blindness.

I've worn glasses since I was sixteen years old, and my sight has only been deteriorating since then. Sadly, vision is something that rarely improves with age. Not that long ago, I was relying on contact lenses (that had the difficult task of helping one eye to see from afar and the other close up) *and* reading glasses. I had countless pairs, stashed all around my house so I would have them on hand every time I needed them. Which was always. And somehow, despite these measures, I *still* couldn't find any glasses when I most needed them!

A few years ago, I went to see my eye doctor. It was just another routine visit—vision tests, eye charts, and that large contraption filled with a million prescriptions lenses. Unfortunately, I had waited a bit too long to make this appointment—I was taking a trip to see my family, and my new contact lens prescription would not be ready by the time I boarded the plane. My doctor, being a gracious man, offered to fit me with some temporary, colored contacts to tide me over until I returned. So I left his office more pleased than otherwise, with the designer hazel lenses I had always wanted.

Three weeks after my trip, I returned to his office and told him I was somehow able to see better than ever. He warned me that my eyes were bound to feel tired soon, and that I would have to eventually switch to my newer, stronger prescription. But I told him it wasn't necessary. I knew I could keep the weaker prescription. I believed God had healed my vision. And He has! I went back to his office months later to ask him for help with my book, as I needed specific information on the properties of the human eye.

A Transcript

Dr.: So those are the basics of optometry …

Me: Thank you so much. Isn't it interesting that God showed me He did something to my physical eyes?

Dr.: Mm hmm …

Me: Because, remember when I met you?

Dr.: Mm hmm …

Me: I had those special contact lenses and also had to have my reading glasses.

Dr.: Mm hmm …

Me: And I still was never able to see very clearly, up close or far away, and felt like I was doomed, but I got used to it.

Dr.: Mm hmm …

Me: So I bought one-dollar reading glasses and placed them all around my house. But now, God wakes me up at three o' clock in the morning, and I have to be able open my eyes and write what He's telling me right away before it's gone.

Dr.: Mm hmm …

Me: That was something I wouldn't have been able to do if I had to try to find my reading glasses.

Dr.: Mm hmm … I think I can explain why you see the way you do.

Me: You can?

His eyes turn to his computer, and he begins typing, looking for my chart. Without removing his eyes from the screen, he continues talking.

Dr.: Well, so far, none of this applies to you. And I think we have you on distance only contacts, is that right?

Me: I have no idea. I only know I like them.

Dr.: Let me look in here …

There are a few seconds of silence. The only sound is the faint clicking of the keyboard.

Dr.: Yeah … your glasses prescription shows a different prescription in each eye, a *significantly* different prescription in each eye. Your contact prescription uses the same lenses in both eyes and neither of them really make sense with what your glasses prescription are. I do not … I do *NOT* understand how you wear those lenses and see all distances clearly.

Me (*looking up close at a book in front of me*): I can read here and … Oh my gosh! I can read the sign behind you written in Spanish!

Dr.: Mm hmm … See? There's not much of an explanation for how you are able to do that with your vision. If your pupils were very small … but they don't appear to be small. Sometimes that could be the case. So I don't know how you do what you do.

Me: It's God!

Dr.: Well, there is definitely … there is no explanation on this page about how you see the way you see.

Me: I know. It's God!

Dr.: I also have to say you are the only person I've met like that. I have no other patients who do what you do.

Me: It's God! It's God!

God showed me He was giving me my physical sight back in order for me to discover my own spiritual blindness. He wanted me to open my soul's eyes. He wanted me to see Him looking back at me.

His Choice

Because God has made us for Himself, our hearts are restless until they rest in Him.

—Saint Augustine of Hippo

Is the human race in the position to understand God's nature? Or is this concept so abstract that we deem it unreachable? The way I see it, God's choice from the beginning has been to establish a relationship with us, His creation.

The divine paradox expresses itself once more in the nature of the Creator in relation to His creation. The Creator fashioned men in His own image (Genesis 1:27). As God's image, we have Godlike attributes. The Spirit of God has shown me the main attribute, which makes us reflect His likeness, is free will. We have a choice in our destiny; a choice made back in Eden. We chose to eat from the Tree of Knowledge of Good and Evil.

When each of us comes into this world, we are subject to external conditions and circumstances that, over time, mold us into the people we are. Place of origin, culture, language, social status, physical makeup, and many other factors come into play. But our lives start taking shape not only according to what we experience, but also what we choose to believe in.

We are all given the chance to make this choice once again: God or not God? Life or death? The Tree of Life or the Tree of Knowledge of Good and Evil? (Deuteronomy 30:19; Joshua 24:15). But God has a choice too, and He made it long ago. God's choice and ultimate will is that we become aware of His existence, and He actively desires to have a relationship with us through the example His Son, Jesus Christ, left for us and by the power of His Holy Spirit. He gave us life in order that we may spend it with Him.

The Arrow of Time

There is so little we really understand about time. Even though humanity has been trying to figure it out since the beginning of time (pun intended), it seems to elude our mortal reason. It has been up for debate in all disciplines of human knowledge, from philosophy to religion and science. Yet a common consensus as to what time actually *is* continues to elude the philosophers, theologians, and men of science.

But the answer seems quite simple to me. Time, in its essence, is simply what God has granted me. I call it life. Time is what I have from the instant I came into existence to the moment I take my last breath. Time is what God has bestowed upon me to make use of my free choice. Time allows me to either draw closer to or away from my Creator. Our precious time is exactly what He wants us to return to Him. He wants our time to be used in the exciting search of our way back to Him. To enhance our spiritual vision, to bask in His light, we must take time to commune with Him, time to worship Him, time to serve Him, time to get to know Him from our human perspective, and time in His hands to become eternal. Time away from Him is wasted and vanishes like vapor in the sunlight.

Back in 1870, an Australian physicist named Ludwig Boltzman came up with the law of entropy—now known as the second law of thermodynamics, one of the most fundamental laws of physics. An easy way to understand entropy is to think of something going from order toward disorder. An ice cube slowly melting in a warm room, a light bulb flickering and eventually burning out, water coming to a rolling boiling on a stove—these are all examples of this destabilization, this change of state. Thanks to the concept of time, we can measure the levels of that change. It is a journey that is considered impossible to reverse; disorder cannot become ordered again, that which has been destabilized and changed cannot go back to its previous state. The one-way, forward-looking direction of entropy is sometimes referred to as the "arrow of time."

If we examined the state of our spiritual entropy, I think we would be shocked. God gave us order and perfection, but our time is running out. The relentless arrow of time is surging forward, and that which He originally gave us is continually disintegrating, never to be regained. And since time is the succession of choices that will bring me back to or away from God, none of it should be wasted. If I want to build a deep relationship with Him, I have to use my time wisely. I have to use it to become aware of His kingdom, of His ways, of His eyes on me, His eyes on my heart.

Our Quest and Our Reward

When I was a child and my father would come back from trip out of town, I just *knew* he'd bring me a present. The second he walked through the door, I would run to him, asking him if he had brought me something. He would nonchalantly answer, "Who me?" or "No, I forgot," but I could tell by the smile on his face that he had a treat for me hidden in one of his pockets. I would look in each and every one of his coat pockets while he tickled me and made me laugh. The real prize was not in the candy or little trinket he had in his pocket. It was in the *relationship;* in the time we spent together playing, tickling, and laughing. He could have just handed me my present with little ado, but instead he yearned for my company and cherished my relationship with him.

Our heavenly Father is the same way. He has so many heavenly gifts for us, so many priceless promises to freely bestow. But He yearns for our relationship with Him. He wants us to spend time with Him, to spend time seeking our spiritual prizes in His Word and in His fellowship. The longer our walk with the Lord and the more attention we lavish on our relationship with Him, the more weapons and artillery we gain to use against our own fleshly desires. It reminds me of a video game my son likes to play—the hero is on a quest and must fight the enemies that appear along the way. As he journeys further toward his goal and vanquishes his attackers, he acquires more tools and weapons.

Our quest is all about growth and relationship. And growth implies movement—cause and effect. God made the choice to give me time, and I have choices as to how I use it. The more time I spend seeking God's light and sharpening my spiritual vision, the more awareness I gain of His reality (Habakkuk

2:14). His will is for us to truly see Him (Ezekiel 39:29), His choice is to reveal Himself to us, and His reward is manifested through the Holy Spirit (Acts 2:17). I am but a small piece of evidence unfolding right before our eyes that the unlearned and ignorant are becoming wise. His choice is to grant wisdom to the simpleminded like myself, to amaze and flabbergast the intellectuals, and to help us all become aware of the power of His Word and to rely on His promises.

A Dream

I have a dream.

I am being born again in His Spirit. I see myself as a tiny, helpless fetus in the hands of God. I am connected to those hands by an umbilical cord. He tells me it is my duty to keep that spiritual umbilical cord healthy, to keep His power flowing into me and strengthening me.

Being Born Into the Light

Everything I once thought I knew
Has fallen into space and disappeared.
My thoughts and ideas
Are hanging from my mind.
They have become so heavy
They crumble down my cheeks,
As tears of stars and galaxies
Fly like robins back into my soul.

Nothing I see makes any sense anymore.
Nothing I once thought stands like before.

When darkness becomes light
And light enters my eyes,
I see strange and unfamiliar forms.
A divine paradox in a still voice tells me,
"Everything is going to be all right."

I'm rushing through the birth canal,
Cold and dark, fear too quick to feel,
Leaving behind old ideas and lies.
And all I hear in the silence is a cosmic scream
Then I SEE myself being born into His hands!

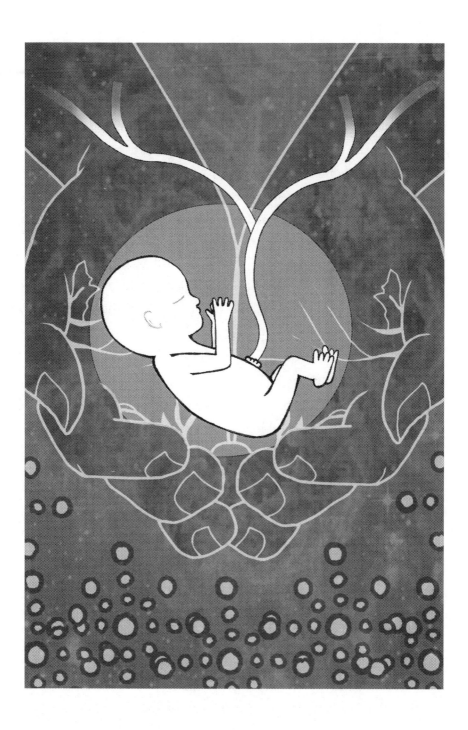

The Cord

Before we are born into the world, we receive nourishment and support from the umbilical cord connecting us to our mother's placenta. The vein in the cord provides our fetal selves with the oxygenated, nutrient-rich blood we need to develop while arteries remove the depleted blood. It is a thoroughly dependent relationship—the fetus cannot survive without the umbilical cord to bring it sustenance and remove impurities. Our spiritual umbilical cord is just as necessary to the development of our relationship with God. In order to be born again, our connection to Him needs to remain healthy and thriving. We need this divine umbilical cord to bring us the spiritually rich promises of the Lord and to remove our own depleted doubts and troubles.

> Finally, brothers, whatever is true, whatever is honorable, whatever is fair, whatever is pure, whatever is acceptable, whatever is commendable, if there is anything of excellence and if there is anything praiseworthy—keep thinking about these things. (Philippians 4:8 ISV)

"Keep thinking about these things." It would be an impossible order were it not for our special, cosmic connection to our Creator. If He did not long for our fellowship, how would we even know what is "pure" or "commendable"? His mind and knowledge are too vast for our brains—no matter how intellectual they may be—to comprehend by themselves. But our souls and spirits are connected to His very being! This connection, this spiritual umbilical cord, is opened when we come to an awareness of Him. It is only then that we may have the spiritual knowledge and wisdom that surpasses all human understanding.

God Makes It All About You

It has always amused me that the English language lacks a differentiation between the singular "you" and the plural "you." The only way to clarify that I am speaking to you plural is if I add a "y'all" or "you guys" to the end of a sentence. God uses the second-person singular when He speaks. He speaks to *you* (singular) because He is a personal God and wants your undivided attention. He longs for us to respond to Him as He reaches for each one of us individually (Psalms 33:15).

It is shocking and amazing that the Creator of the entire cosmos—whose power fashioned the stars and the heavens and placed them in perfect order in the universe—has also crafted me, His simple and amazed Grace. But it's true! Each one of us is unique and essentially one-of-a-kind. Your heavenly Father handcrafted you with your inimitable personality and talents and ordained your birth from your mother's womb (Psalm 71:6; Psalm 139:14). And as your Creator, He has a unique purpose for you that only *you* can accomplish.

God made the choice to pursue a relationship with us … but the maintenance of that bond, the pursuit of that relationship, is up to us. Our duty is to see that we let *nothing* distract us from that connection. Only an authentic relationship with God will promote authentic relationships with other people.

Your Focus, Your Choice

It is not always easy to make our relationship with Him our top priority. Today, more than ever, we can hardly get a break from distractions. We have to learn *to* focus, we have to learn *when* to focus, and we have to learn upon *what* to focus.

Focus is not a value treasured by our modern world. It is not a coincidence that, just when science is bringing us closer to the evidence of a Creator, we have to deal with the hundreds (if not millions) of daily data shots to our brains. Whether you're watching a movie, spending time at a family reunion, or eating dinner at a fancy restaurant, chances are you'll see more than one person there who's trying to do those things with a cell phone permanently attached to their hand. Usually, they're even texting more than one person at a time! Between smartphones, the Internet, television, and social media, we are losing our single-mindedness. The battle for our attention is being intensified by the minute. It's like something is pulling us away from the possibility of becoming aware of God's reality.

There is only one way to overcome the distractions: We have to question everything that does not pertain to our private, personal relationship with Him. *Everything*—including our religious affiliations and theological opinions. We are responsible, first and foremost, for our own salvation. God will not ask you if your friends loved Him or if you only hung around those who did. He will not ask you if you belonged to such-and-such denomination or if you followed the religion of your forefathers by the letter of the law.

It didn't matter to Jesus what the world at large thought of him. He once looked Peter in the eye and asked him, " 'But what about you?' he asked. 'Who do *you* say I am?' Peter answered,

'You are the Christ' " (Mark 8:29). Jesus wanted the personal opinion of someone in a relationship with Him. Only *you* will stand in front of God on the day of judgment. And the questions will not be about the good deeds you performed or how holy you were or how many times a week you attended church. They will be about the way you chose to love God and your level of awareness of His kingdom reality (Hebrews 8:10–11). It is, after all, about you and God. When you place that relationship above everything else in your life, the rest will fall into place.

Question everything, even what you read in this book. Find out about things on your own. Rely on your amazing connection to the Holy Spirit for revelation. Turn your back on the set paradigms that may be limiting your spiritual vision and blocking your connection to the Lord. Read your Bible, savor it and absorb its promises and wisdom. Let the words come alive in you, and let them transform you into His likeness. His choice has already been made. He loves us. He wants us. He pursues us.

Is that what *you* want?

His Reality

To be or not to be. That is the question.

—William Shakespeare

There is no denying we exist in a world we cannot fully understand, a world filled with paradoxes. If we were to take an imaginary journey into the core of what we perceive as matter (which our senses have told us is "reality"), we would find ourselves in a realm of infinite possibilities and uncertainty, mesmerized and searching for answers. If reality is not what our senses perceive, what the heck is it? The search for an ultimate and objective reality has sent us scurrying in a million theoretical directions, but it all ends up coming back to us. As individuals. We each have to make a subjective decision as to what reality truly is.

The way I see it, there are no words in any language eloquent enough to explain God's reality. Concepts like "time," "love," and "God" boggle our tiny brains, so we decide to not think too much about them and rely on the false illusion that the things around us are the way they are supposed to be. We wake up in the morning, go to work, make a living, come back, go to bed—and do it all over again, day after day. But deep inside, we all have a profound longing to find out who we really are and if there is a purpose to our lives. We have an insatiable need to know what is real.

He is reality. He is the I AM, and I have the choice to be or not to be. When I choose to transform myself into His likeness, I choose to *be*. When I decide to operate under His holy light, I am no longer blind. My spiritual eyes are wide open, and I can see the connection between God and every one of us. My brain is able to understand the spiritual realities around me. And then I am able to move from my reality into His.

What Is Reality?

When they were young, science and religion got into quarrels and needed to be separated until they learned to play nice. Mankind separated science from religion as we separated mind from body and soul from spirit. Most of us still flinch when we hear people talking about time, gravity, quantum physics, string theory, and so on; much less in the same conversation as God's kingdom. We've been taught to judge such subjects as "new age" or "mystic" and not fit for discussion among God's people.

I, too, had doubts. When God's Spirit compelled me to start researching concepts like gravity, quantum physics, and black holes, I asked Him whether I should be researching more spiritual-sounding ideas. Surely words like *faith, humility,* and *pride* would be more suitable, I thought. But now I can finally see where He was going.

Discoveries in quantum physics have proven that there is another order of reality that lies beneath that which we know. As a matter of fact, it has opened the doors wide to the idea that what we may perceive as "real" (the physical world) may not be, and that what we perceive as an abstract idea (God) may be the only source of ultimate reality. In the answer to the most important question, "What is reality?" science and faith have come together at last. There are no more excuses, no more places to hide. The false dichotomy that has pitted the material world against the spiritual has been shattered. We have the opportunity to exercise our freedom of choice with a deeper consciousness of what knowledge is available to us right now, today. Through an interpenetration of psychology, science, physics, and religion, mankind has come to a crossroad. A more realistic, multifaceted concept of God has been presented to us, and we have a choice to make.

The Age of Accountability

The spiritual history of mankind can be likened to the growth of a child. Born helpless newborns, we have now grown up enough to be held accountable for our actions. God has been so gracious and understanding with our lack of maturity and knowledge! Our global human understanding has been evolving this entire time—to deny this would be like asserting the Earth is flat. But the Spirit of God has revealed to me that a much deeper, more intentional focus is now required. He longs for our eyes to watch Him, our minds to rest in His, and our hearts to find shelter in the light of His reality. He longs for us to have faith. "Now faith is a well-grounded assurance of that for which we hope, and a conviction of the *reality* of things, which we do not see" (Hebrews 11:1, emphasis added).

Having faith is my choice. Having faith means I have sharpened my spiritual vision, made the choice to let His light illuminate me, and have approached what I see as reality with utter humility. Having faith means I have learned to see His eyes watching me and have made a commitment to strengthening my relationship with Him. Having faith means I am ready to see *His* reality.

A Dream

I have a dream.

I see the distorted circle where humankind dwells. It is foggy, shaky, unstable, and unpredictable. It is walled by envy, rejection, selfishness, fear, lust, idolatry, dissatisfaction, hopelessness, self-indulgence, darkness, unforgiveness, and sin. It has a strong stench of pride.

People are pushing and pulling and snatching at one another. They are climbing stairs that go nowhere, walking through tunnels without end, and boating on lakes of despair and loneliness. They are unhappy.

Some are eating themselves to death; others are buying things and carrying their heavy possessions on their shoulders like pack mules. There is loud music; people dance to distract themselves from the agony, hide their suffering, and to drown out the cries of those who have been abused and abandoned.

Then, some of them bow down in repentance. In their desperation and humility, they become small enough to fall "up" through a passage leading to God's reality.

This is a perfect sphere and has the aroma of love and acceptance. I can see the love of God reflected in those who serve the weak. People seem to know and understand their purpose for being. They carry their eyes in their hearts rather than in their heads. I can see the notes of the music playing in the background, and they look like hope, forgiveness, joy, mercy, compassion, trust, mercy, and gentleness.

His Kingdom

Moving from our reality into His makes us citizens of His kingdom.

The journey is a divine paradox—simple, but not easy. We have to leave *all* behind, to dispossess ourselves of anything that might weigh us down. We cannot carry our material possessions, our old goals, preconceived ideas, or religious pride with us. There's just no room for them! If your sense of worth depends on those sorts of things, you are not yet ready to make the trip. God never gave us those things in the first place. He will supply everything you need for the journey. How could He not? He is the Creator of all! The world did not start with a big bang, but with His quiet whisper. Sir Isaac Newton wrote in his *Principia Mathematica* (1687):

> This most beautiful system of the sun, planets, and comets could only proceed from the counsel and dominion of an intelligent and powerful Being. And if the fixed stars are the centers of other like systems, these, being formed by the like wise counsel, must be all subject to the dominion of One, especially since the light of the fixed stars is of the same nature with the light of the sun and from every system light passes into all the other systems; and lest the systems of the fixed stars should, by their gravity, fall on each other mutually, he hath placed those systems at immense distances from one another.
>
> This Being governs all things not as the soul of the world, but as Lord over all; and on account of his dominion he is wont to be called "Lord God" ... or "Universal Ruler."

(I have the audacity to add to that list of honorifics. He also wants to be called: the Singularity Point of Creation; Ultimate Reality; Perfect and Absolute Consciousness, Love, and Creative Power; Observer and Participator; and Constant Factor K).

God's spiritual kingdom is reflected in the physiognomy of this world and the universe. The Creator did not intend for us to arrogantly assume we are the only form of life in the whole universe. He wanted us to inculcate a sense of humility, to be aware of the fragility of our existence.

Looking up to the galaxies should humble *us*. Looking down to the atom should magnify *God*.

If Jesus had lived in our time rather than His own, I can visualize Him crafting parables to explain His kingdom. They would be a little different than the ones that speak of loaves and fishes. For example,

"Think of my Father's kingdom as a singularity point, where time and space cease to exist. Where reality comes in and out of existence to defy human understanding. He is at the center of everything that has been created, and it will be the end of all reality as you know it."

I'm ready to dive into all the possibilities held together by one singular point. Why would I choose otherwise? My own reality is but a dim reflection of His.

A Road Map to Reality

In this book, I've been essentially tracing out a route to God's reality. I have been reliving my journey to the understanding of Him that I now have. The steps are pretty simple.

First, we must acknowledge that:

- **We are born spiritually blind:** 2 Thessalonians 2:1; John 9; Isaiah 44:18; Ezekiel 12:2; Psalm 135:6; Ephesians 2:1, 5; Colossians 2:13
- **We become servants to our own flesh if we choose not to see:** Psalm 69:23; Isaiah 6:10; 29:10; 41:29; 2 Peter 2:10; Galatians 5:13; 6:8; Romans 6:18–19
- **We are nothing but a vapor, a shapeless image:** James 4:14; Psalm 39:6
- **We are not gods or as wise as we think we are:** 1 Corinthians 1:20–21; 2:14; 3:19; 4:6; Ecclesiastes 3:11
- **We are not our own masters:** Acts 7:40; Exodus 32:23; Ecclesiastes 3:11; Proverbs 8:23
- **We have no life until we choose to accept Him:** 1 John 1:2; John 3:36

Fortunately, we are:
- **Created in His image:** Ephesians 4:24; Genesis 5:1
- **Given an individual choice:** Matthew 8:13; 9:22, 28–29; Psalm 139:13

To exercise this choice, we must:
- **Accept the fact we are created beings:** (It takes full amounts of humility) Genesis 1:27; Colossians 1:16; Revelation 4:11
- **Take responsibility for our own blindness:** 2 Peter 1:9; 1 John 1:6; 2:9–11; 3:15; 4:20
- **Dress ourselves with godly humility for the battle:** Luke 17:21; Matthew 11:29; Proverbs 18:12; 22:4; 29:23; Colossians 2:18–23; Ephesians 4:2
- **Try to make sense of time:** Ecclesiastes 3:1–14; 9:9

- **Choose to see though our faith:** Hebrews 11; Galatians 3:23; James 2:22; Romans 4:16; Luke 8:10

When we do these things we will understand that:
- **He is the I AM:** Exodus 3:14; Isaiah 46:9
- **He is the ultimate reality:** Colossians 2:17
- **He is life:** John 1:4; 10:10; 1 John 5:12
- **And we will not comprehend until we see the complete circle of His divine paradox:** Ecclesiastes 11:5

That's it! That's the road map. But how will this journey end?

This book does not have an ending. You can finish it any way you choose. I have.

How It All Started

It all started with words.

A few short years ago, I was content being a wife and mother and served God as well as I could. I taught Bible classes, went on mission trips, and used my real estate license to help people in need. But I made a decision to say yes to whatever God had in mind for my life, and since then the cascade of events has left me unable to deny His involvement. Coincidences and random, perfectly staged situations became the norm in my daily life. And He began giving me *words,* seemingly random words that I knew must hold some significance. My mission was to research and study them and write about what I learned.

At first, I thought words like *gravity* and *quantum physics* had no place in the spiritual realm, that they had no relevance in what He was trying to teach me. Now I *see*. I know that isn't the case. He has woven each word, each concept, in such a divine and beautiful way to show me the grandiose reality of reality itself.

I have kicked and screamed all the way here. You cannot imagine how many times I have fought with the Spirit, whining about my inadequacies to write this book. But that's what happens when you choose the foolish things of the world. Even in my wildest dreams, I never imagined He would take me on a trip as wild and intense as this one. Two and a half years ago, all I had was random words with no correlation among them at all. Now I have filled five journals and hundreds of loose papers, napkins, and notes with nuggets of God's wisdoms and insights. Taking heed of the promptings of the Spirit and asking Him questions, I received my responses through dreams, websites, books, and visions. I started to discover truths I had never seen before. He was looking for an empty vessel, and He found me to be empty and willing to be used.

So here I am. Presenting this book to you, who has chosen to read it. The message is simple: GOD IS! There is a reality far more real that what our senses can perceive.

Goad

"And he said, 'Who are you, Lord?' And the Lord said, 'I am Jesus whom you persecute: it is hard for you to kick against the *goads*'" (Acts 9:5 KJV, emphasis added).

After happening upon the above verse, I found myself on a three-day, mind-blowing trip, trying to grasp the hidden meaning of the word *goad*—a word usually shunned as unimportant by many translations and Bible commentaries.

The dictionary definition of the word is multi-pronged. Primarily, a goad is defined as "a stick with a pointed or electrically charged end, for driving cattle, oxen, etc." (The image of prodding a reluctant or lazy creature is ripe for spiritual analogy, isn't it?).

> The words of the wise are like goads, their collected sayings like firmly embedded nails—given by one Shepherd. Be warned, my son, of anything in addition to them. Of making many books there is no end, and much study wearies the body. Now all has been heard; here is the conclusion of the matter: Fear God and keep his commandments, for this is the whole [duty] of man. For God will bring every deed into judgment, including every hidden thing, whether it is good or evil. (Ecclesiastes 12:11–12)

The second definition describes the reaction that pointed stick might incur. "Something that encourages, urges, or drives," the dictionary continues. "A stimulus." Words of wisdom from the faithful, the word of the Lord, the circumstances of our lives—all of these things can act as goads in our quest to follow God's path.

My Goad

Now, as I finish this book, God has seen fit—in His multifold wisdom—to allow me go through a cancer scare. I was recently diagnosed with Stage Two ovarian cancer and have dealt with the wild array of emotions news like this brings about. But the debris of my fears and insecurities has been cleared away, and I can clearly *see* what He is up to. He wants to give me more material to write about. He has placed the big guns in my hands. Now I have to truly experience everything I'm trying to communicate through this book.

After my diagnosis, a million suggestions of cures, treatments, and coping mechanisms flooded my inbox, onto my Facebook wall, and right to my doorstep. I am blessed that so many people love me and want to help me fight this uninvited guest in my life. But I am *not* undergoing chemotherapy at this time. Until the Spirit of God tells me differently, I will choose the path of utter and absolute humility. Meanwhile, my choice lacks eye-evidence. The people who love me don't necessarily understand. It is so much easier to believe in something our eyes can see, like chemotherapy and its consequences. It is much harder to have total faith in God, to believe that He knows what He's doing.

I feel like Job. He survived some truly terrible calamities. He was inundated with well-meaning advice. And when he finally came face-to-face with God, he became aware that through all of those struggles, God was trying to reveal Himself as all-powerful and all-wise; a God whose ways are unimpeachable, loving, and merciful.

> Then Job replied to the LORD: "I know that you can do all things; no plan of yours can be thwarted. You asked, 'Who is this that obscures my counsel without knowledge?' Surely I spoke of things I did not understand, things too wonderful for me to know. You said, 'Listen now, and I will speak; I will question you, and you shall answer me.' My ears had heard of you but now my eyes have seen you. (Job 42:1–5)

The cancer is nothing but a goad, urging me onward to Him. It pricks me, motivates me, and wakes me up. It is a catalyst for my life, and I will surely not kick against it. Knowing and becoming fully aware that I live only by the grace of God is a blessing. It helps me to live with so much more intensity and authenticity, and I am so thankful for it. I will let God do His work in me. Even if the end is not what I want or expect, I have total trust in Him. I know He has it all under control.

Sidenote

As this book goes to publication, I am starting chemotherapy. It hasn't been a quick decision; I've been thinking about it for over nine months, and I can truly say my decision to begin was out of love and obedience—not fear.

I wrote this book about "seeing" and overcoming fears. Now more than ever, I am having to rely on my faith in God as I remember my own words.

There can be no doubt that cancer destroys the normalcy of life. However, it is my choice to decide if it is an attack to my flesh or a goad to my spirit. Do I duck in an attempt to miss the assault? Or do I open my spiritual eyes and see it for what it really is? Like a ball of kryptonite thrown directly at me, I will not fear. The many blessings and lessons that will be learned throughout this coming phase are so much more real to me. Therefore, I have decided to claim James 1:2–4:

> Consider it pure joy, my brothers, whenever you
> face trials of many kinds, because you know that
> the testing of your faith develops perseverance.

Perseverance must finish its work so that you may
be mature and complete, not lacking anything.

A good friend helped me to see that for me personally it will take more faith to go through the chemotherapy than not. I am more afraid of the treatment than I am of dying. I am not attached to anything on this earth because I have already given it all up to God, but because many people around me love me and need to see me fighting to stay alive for them, I am.

God knows my heart, and He will not let me go through this without teaching me valuable lessons and a more transcending purpose than I could ever dream. The question has changed from "Why Cancer"? to "How Cancer"? How is this cancer going to be used for the glory of God?

Whatever the outcome, I know God will not waste the pain and anguish that lie ahead for me and my family and friends. I visualize a long and dark tunnel, but there is a bright light at the end. So I move toward it and hold these words from my son Kenny close to my heart. "Mom, you'll be fine. I know. Because even though your body is obviously deteriorating, I know God never takes anything away from you without giving something even better back. So if your body is deteriorating, it can only mean your spirit is about to get much stronger." And who in their right mind and spirit would be afraid of it? Oh, what a blessing!

Appendix:
Tidbits, Nuggets, and
Butterfly Kisses

These are the little smithereens of God's wisdom that would wake me up in the middle of the night. I'd write them down as soon as I got them. They were like lighting bugs—I had to catch them fast, otherwise I'd lose them. It taught me immediate obedience. Others came up as I talked to people, and I had to write them down because I am a firm believer that everything good belongs to Him.

The way I see it, things of God are best said with the least words. It is, after all, a matter of the heart. Read them slowly. Savor and enjoy!

- Understanding God's mind may be a difficult task, but we can know His heart.

- It's funny—we are constantly asking for signs, but if we ever get a glimpse of one, we quickly look away and renounce it for fear of being called "crazy."
- Understanding God's knowledge is veiled with a paradoxical nature that defies human logic.
- Lord, open your arms wide 'cause I am running to You before my fears catch up with me.
- In light of my willpower, I choose His *power* and know He *will*.
- My pride tastes bitter when I swallow it but becomes so sweet when it reaches my soul.
- I wish I could make my words dance to the rhythm of the music I'm hearing in my soul.
- Walk closely in total trust right behind Him so all you can see is His back. You will never be afraid of what lies ahead.
- I am falling in love *with* God as much as I am falling *on* God.
- I will never be able to give You anything more than You have already given me in the first place.
- My life is my journey back to You.
- You dressed me with humility when You found me naked with pride.
- You are growing me small.
- I can smell the sweet aroma of Your love.
- Who wants logic and normality when you can have God-thought?
- His Word contains the residue of His breath, the same breath that breathed us into existence.
- You don't want anything *from* me but *for* me.

- Bead every second of my life to make a jewel unto Your eyes.
- The battle is won in your head first.
- It is not history as much as it is His story.
- There is freedom in submission, power in humility.
- My life is death if not in Yours.
- Destiny is not the reward but the outcome of the journey.
- I heard Him whispering when I was a child. I heard Him speaking to me as a young woman. I hear Him singing in my old age.
- An insight is nothing more than *in* sight.
- I am not amaz*ing* Grace but amaz*ed* Grace.
- Lord, help us not fool ourselves into thinking we are fooling you.
- Nobody has ever died perfect.
- It has always been about our heart.
- We resemble the Father when we carry His eyes in our hearts.
- He is the LIGHT so we can SEE
  He is the TRUTH so we can KNOW
  He is the WAY se we can WALK
  He is the LIFE so we can LIVE!
- He owns the trademark of "good."
- We are a reflection of the Maker. Spiritual beings wrapped up in flesh, gravitating to their own hollow satisfaction.
- I choose to hang onto Him so close that the winds of this world wont be able to snatch me away.
- Don't allow God's work to take you away from God's heart and fellowship.

- I'm losing my mind in exchange of His.
- I have found God. Or is it that I have chosen to be found by Him?
- Let me drink of Your wisdom and eat of Your words to let them be part of my inner being.
- Life has a better view when you're in His Hands.
- His kingdom is hidden in plain sight for those willing to *see.*
- I claim no wisdom of my own other than the wisdom granted to me by the Spirit of God. There is no room for pride when you realize He uses You because you are "empty."
- Sometimes a divine paradox ordains that godliness can only be understood by the simple and humble in heart (1 Corinthians 2:9–16).
- Sometimes I don't do what others think I ought to do but what I believe needs to get done.
- Your eyes went out looking for a foolish one to use, and You found me.
- Divine paradox: I have no other value to offer to the world but the fact that You talk to me.
- I am committed even if I get committed in the process.
- When you become aware of the power of God in you, you learn to live in permanent victory and trust. Even IF.
- I am a simple and amazed messenger of His supernatural power.
- It is so hard finding someone worth following on Twitter. Doesn't Jesus tweet?

- We miss out on so many miracles because we rather take matter into our hands.
- Knowledge without God breeds pride. Knowledge of God is wisdom.
- A divine paradox in the spiritual realm is perfectly reflected as an optical illusion. If you observe it intently and with consciousness, you will **see.**
- Difficult circumstances are strategically placed in your life to reveal your true relationship with God.
- Weeds do grow taller than grass, but they are weeds nevertheless.
- Don't let your heart be led by your eyes.
- We understand grace better when we give it.
- He brings you godly peace within yourself by struggles, tribulation, and war.
- Insights come to me without words, and it is my job to dress them up in order to present them to the world.
- I am a long way from knowing what I am doing. Thus, to God be all the glory!
- God has not revealed to me any new concepts, only a better interpretation of them.
- I may be falling apart, but He is catching every piece of me in His hands.
- I am so simpleminded and lighthearted that it makes me almost retarded.
- He took me seriously when I was five years old—proof that *time* does not matter.
- As a child, I understood there was nothing I could do for Him to love me more or less. It gave me the

freedom to just rest in His peace and love Him that much more passionately.

- When I was five, I stood in front of a crucifix and told Jesus, "I'll spend the rest of my life wiping off your tears and making your boo-boos feel better."
- I pray with my eyes open and sing with my eyes closed.
- My lack of memory keeps me from lying, and it gives God a clean slate to work with everyday.
- I do not lie, but I am often in state of confusion.
- Fear distorts reality.
- Home is not where I come from anymore but where I long to go.
- God has a way to measure my pH level—peace and hope—to determine the state of my faith in Him.
- I do not have enough information on the matter to voice an opinion.
- There is something inside of me that knows more than I do.
- Science will ultimately prove the evidence of God.
- Don't let your fear stand in the way of a miracle.
- I am an instrument that has chosen to be played by the Master Musician. Listen to the music.
- One day you will be asked to FACE *the* BOOK! (Revelation 20:15)
- I've learned to keep moving by obedience, not expectation of the results.
- The problem does not lie in the circumstances but in our *reaction* to them.
- Free will is something we either hold onto or pour out.
- I have nothing worth offering to Him but my life.

- Live like you are loved!
- A humble heart is a thankful heart; a thankful heart is a humble heart.
- I may be corky, tacky, and cheesy, but He loves me anyway.
- There is nothing like letting go and falling straight on love.
- I will not let opinions become the basis for my beliefs.
- God does not need our acknowledgment to BE. We do.
- God *is*. We choose to be or not to be.
- My attitude defines the color of the outside world in my eyes.
- Truth exists apart from my understanding, acceptance, or recognition of it. So does God.
- I am seeking the *King* to *see.*
- Happiness has a way of catching up with you when you are on your knees washing someone else's feet.
- Happiness is in pursuit of you. STOP. Be still, and KNOW He is God.
- In my younger years, it was so hard for me to lay my troubles at Your feet until I found out what You did with them. Now, Father, I run to You!
- I have learned not to be tossed around by my feelings and emotions but to stand firm by what I *know.*
- Sin tastes as good as cheese tastes to the mouse eating it from a trap.
- Difficult situations are only an illusion of what is going to come about from the experience if you let it.
- Anything beyond supplying a need is greed and a distraction.

- Let your attitude be a reflection of your choices and not your circumstances.
- The silver lining on the clouds can only be seen if the Son is behind them.
- You will never be able to give God more than what He already has given you in the first place.
- I can walk in the dark with the assurance that with every step I take, His hands will be there to catch me.
- It is not about the destiny itself but the shape we are in when we get there.
- Let the journey shape you into your destiny.
- Be still and know that I am God so *My* glory and majesty may be reflected in *your* perfect peace and trust.
- Some people cover themselves with riches, power, and intellect because they are afraid to be seen naked in the eyes of God.
- Truth is like running water: You can't hold it, own it, or claim it. You can only drink it and let it become part of your inner being.
- Accept opposition in your life as building blocks to your own shelter where you keep safe your heart.
- It seems to me that the older I get the more instincts I lose. I have to become more conscious in order to survive.
- All I can pray is that beauty may move into my heart since it is fading from my face.
- Attentive observations of patterns can lead us to truths hidden around us.
- Blind us so we can finally *see* You.

- My God holds my soul in His hands and calms it with butterfly kisses.
- Do not lure me into talking about "God things" unless you are ready to be tied up for a while.
- Sometimes it is best to not know all the rules and let your imagination fly.
- I float on a pool of uncertainty with my faith in my heart so I won't drown.
- Godly humility is displayed in obedience.
- Why is it that we exercise our freedom in the don'ts and not in the yesses?
- I am aware I may be the smallest fish in the pond. Yet God still has His eye on me.
- A humble heart is a heart that *sees*.
- I will never follow my heart again unless You are holding it in Your hands.
- He has chosen an unlikely character like me to accentuate His character!
- When do coincidences cease to be coincidences?
- I don't need a truth to only believe in. I need a truth to live in!
- God is utterly AWEmazing!
- God will stretch me like a string in a violin—just tight enough to make music with my life.
- We are seeking a mathematical explanation for matters much higher than numbers.
- Humanity is good at taking things apart and analyzing them but never good enough to put them back together.
- Science thrives on the *hope* that one day they'll find an *answer*.

Faith thrives on the *assurance* that one day they we will be *one* with it.

- We undermine the manifold complexity of God.
- Science does not deny the existence of God. That is an individual choice.
- True humility is looking in the mirror and seeing nothing but your own faults being vanished by the overpowering Spirit of God.
- When I acknowledge my insignificance, I discover His greatness.
- He has given us time. He would like for us to reciprocate.
- Our own choices can give us freedom or imprisonment forever.
- His Word is planted in the fertile soil of our hearts to produce fruit in His perfect timing.
- You cannot really believe God and be unchanged.
- My judgment feature is soon to be deleted. May God help me not to judge those who judge.
- His words are being tattooed deep in my soul.
- One of my purposes in life is to hypostatize God's reality to the world.
- We need to learn to *love* people into the kingdom and not judge them.
- God has given me the astounding opportunity to transcend into His cosmic consciousness. I'm taking the quest, flying on the wings of humility.
- Taking a watch apart will not give you an understanding of the nature of its maker.
- About the Big Bang—I know the Big; can't say I recognize the Bang.

- The God Factor is the "K" that dissolves all divine paradoxes.
- I believe it is no longer me trying to do the will of God but rather the will of God freely flowing through me to testify of His own power and glory.
- The first reformation was to put the Bible back in the hands of His people. Now the struggle is to move it into their hearts and minds.
- We still fight a daily battle, but the war has already been won.
- The clearer I recognize my sin, the clearer my eyes see Your grace.
- My future smells like God. It is His will I have blazing in my heart.
- Emotions move me no more. It is Your will alone.
- Some words must be experienced in order to be really understood.
- I have been wrong before when I was convinced I was right. What would make me think I'm right now? Uncertainty keeps me humble.
- The gift has been granted, salvation has been delivered, the debt has been paid ... Your move.